Interpreting the political

This book uses techniques of analysis derived from semiotics and linguistics to challenge assumptions about the neutrality of language in the construction of 'the political'. The breadth of methodologies used is extensive, but each Chapter also tackles a substantive political issue. Collectively, the contributors to this work offer new interpretations of political events and phenomena including:

- the socio-linguistic construction of 'the self' and 'identity';
- the symbolic power of national anthems;
- discourses of sexual politics;
- the role of the researcher in fieldwork;
- the 'Hill–Thomas' hearings.

The combination of methodological pluralism rooted in concrete political issues makes this an exciting and original contribution to the field of political theory and the study of politics more generally.

Terrell Carver is a Professor of Political Theory, University of Bristol. **Matti Hyvärinen** is a Research Fellow, University of Tampere, Finland.

Interpreting the political

New methodologies

Edited by Terrell Carver and
Matti Hyvärinen

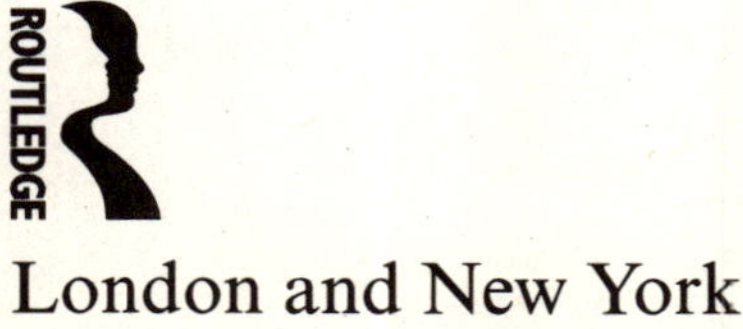

London and New York

First published 1997
by Routledge
11 New Fetter Lane, London EC4P 4EE

Simultaneously published in the USA and Canada
by Routledge
29 West 35th Street, New York, NY 10001

Typeset in Times by Routledge
Printed and bound in Great Britain by T.J. International Ltd,
Padstow, Cornwall

British Library Cataloguing in Publication Data
A catalogue record for this book is available from the British Library

Library of Congress Cataloguing in Publication Data
Interpreting the political : new methodologies / edited by Terrell
  Carver and Matti Hyvärinen.
    p.   cm.
  Includes bibliographical references and index.
  1. Political science–Methodology.   I. Carver, Terrell.
  II. Hyvärinen, Matti.
  JA71.I58   1997
  324´ .072–dc20   96–9857
                                                               CIP

ISBN 0–415–13194–4 (hbk)
ISBN 0–415–13195–2 (pbk)

Contents

Notes on contributors

Josef Bleicher teaches in the Department of Social Sciences at Glasgow Caledonian University. He is of German origin and has published extensively on philosophy of scientific methodology and hermeneutics, notably *Contemporary Hermeneutics* and *The Hermeneutic Imagination*. He is currently involved in cross-national studies on the way that 'Europe' is discursively constructed and interpreted politically.

Valerie Bresnihan is currently working in the Equality Studies Centre, University College, Dublin. Her present research concerns the symbolic structure of thought associated with the Irish political system. Her other academic interests extend to studies of prisoners and the prison system in Ireland, and she is shortly to begin a research project on symbolic structures in that field. She is also chairperson of the Irish Penal Reform Trust.

Terrell Carver is a graduate of Columbia University, New York, took two graduate degrees at the University of Oxford, and has been working at English universities since 1974. Currently he is Professor of Political Theory at the University of Bristol, and is on the editorial board for MEGA, the Marx–Engels collected works. He has published extensively in that area, in philosophy of social science, and most recently in gender studies.

James Der Derian is Professor in the Political Science Department at the University of Massachusetts at Amherst, specialising in international relations. He is a graduate of McGill University in Montreal, and has two graduate degrees from the University of Oxford. He has published extensively on postmodern political theory, diplomacy and anti-diplomacy, and the role of computer technology in national security culture.

Matti Hyvärinen is Research Fellow at the University of Tampere, Finland. Moving between political science and sociology, he has researched and published on social movements, including two books on the Finnish student movement, using autobiographical methodology and theories of rhetoric. He is currently working on the conceptual history of Finnish political culture.

Marja Keränen has a Ph.D. from the University of Jyvaskyla, and is Senior Researcher of the Finnish Academy there. She has published on political science and gender, and has recently done fieldwork in Britain, based at the University of Manchester and the LSE. Her current project, with Josef Bleicher, deals with the rhetoric of peripheralisation in the context of European integration.

Véronique Mottier is of Dutch/Swiss background, and has a degree in political science from the University of Geneva. From 1989 to 1993 she was Assistant Lecturer in Political Science there, and since then has been on an extended sabbatical leave to complete her Ph.D. on 'Subjectivity and social theory' at the University of Cambridge. She has published articles on Foucault, sexual politics and direct democracy.

Kari Palonen is Professor of Political Science at the University of Jyvaskyla. He teaches political theory and rhetoric, and is also a board member of the nationwide graduate school in political science and coordinator of the Scandinavian network in conceptual history. Besides publishing a study of Sartre's conception of politics, he has edited a book on 'texts, contexts and concepts' and another on 'reading the political'.

Klaus Sondermann has an MA from the Erlangen University in Germany, and a doctorate in social science from the University of Jyvaskyla, Finland. He is research fellow at the Research Institute for Social Sciences at the University of Tampere there, and is an editor of *Associations*, a journal for social and legal theory. He has published on nationalism, racism and ethnic relations.

Acknowledgements

An earlier version of Chapter 2 appeared in Terrell Carver, *Gender is Not a Synonym for Women*: ' "He said/she said": interpreting the Clarence Thomas–Anita Hill Hearings', pp. 101–18. Copyright © 1996 by Lynne Rienner Publishers, Inc. Used with permission of the publisher.

An earlier version of Chapter 3 appeared as 'Käänteen ja jat Kuvuuden retoriikka: Anu Rantasen tarina', Chapter 4 of Matti Hyvärinen, *Viimeiset taistot* (Tampere: Vastapaino, 1994). Used with permission of the publisher.

Earlier versions of Chapter 4 appeared as Véronique Mottier, 'La mise en discours de la sexualité: le féminisme à la recherche des stratégies', *Swiss Yearbook of Political Science 1994*, 34: 79–98, and Véronique Mottier, 'The politics of sex: truth games and the Hite Reports', *Economy and Society* (a Routledge journal), vol. 24, no. 4 (November 1995), pp. 520–39. Used with permission of the publishers.

A similar version of Chapter 10 appeared as James Der Derian, *Social Text*, no. 24 (Spring 1990), pp. 187–92. Used with permission of the author.

Individual authors would like to express personal thanks as follows:

- Chapter 4 (Véronique Mottier). 'Earlier versions were presented to the ECPR Annual Session of Workshops in Limerick, 30 March to 3 April 1992, as well as to the 2nd Foucault and Politics Conference on "Alternative political imaginations: the logics of contestation", Goldsmiths College, University of London, 8–9 April 1994. I would like to thank participants in both events, as well as Anthony Giddens, Kate Nash, Nikolas

Rose and an anonymous reader for *Economy and Society*, for their useful comments and criticisms. I also thank David Mikosz and John Sutcliffe for their help with linguistic improvements of the text. I am also grateful to the Swiss National Science Foundation, the Société Académique de Genève and the Schmidheiny Foundation for their generous financial support of my Ph.D research, on which this Chapter is based, at the University of Cambridge.

- Chapter 5 (Valerie Bresnihan). 'I wish to record my sincere thanks to John Baker, Iseult Honahan, Attracta Inghram and Tim Mooney for taking the time out from their busy lives to read this chapter. Their comments have greatly improved the final draft.'
- Chapter 7 (Kari Palonen). 'I am grateful to Josef Bleicher for translating passages from the chapter on Norway that are present in Enzensberger's *Ach Europa!* but omitted from the English translation *Europe, Europe.*'
- The editors would like to express their gratitude to the European Consortium for Political Research, which sponsored a workshop on 'Applying new interpretive methodologies', held at the University of Limerick, Ireland, frm 30 March to 4 April 1992. Chapters 2–9 originated as papers presented and discussed on this occasion.

1   Introduction

Terrell Carver and Matti Hyvärinen

This book aims to further the new methodological pluralism in political science and political studies by employing interpretive methodologies. In particular, this collection brings a uniquely Continental perspective to an English-speaking audience. While much in the approach and substance of these papers will be familiar, some aspects will strike English-speaking readers from a fresh angle. A number of different intellectual and national traditions of research are represented among the authors in this volume, ranging from native Finnish through German-speaking Central European and on to expatriate Dutch. As authors are not inscriptions of their institutions, birthplaces or places of residence, we hasten to add that 'point of view' is not necessarily predictable from institutional or national associations. But the authorial voices in the collection do display different ways of theorising, different kinds of theory and different sorts of illustrative experience.

The editors would like to draw particular attention to the unusual range and synthesis of research methods and strategies employed in the chapters that follow. Moreover they would also like to urge Anglo-American and other English-speaking readers to make an intellectual and imaginative effort to interpret, and not merely reject as 'foreign' or 'Continental', the arguments and insights that other intellectual traditions and personally conceptualised approaches have to offer. For example, political science, or political studies, in non-Anglo-Saxon traditions may be more closely allied to, or even derived from, areas of study such as psychology or anthropology, than is likely to be the case for most Anglo-American readers of this volume. Assumptions about the researcher as writer or as political actor may also be somewhat altered from those familiar in the UK and US.

Reading this collection is therefore a way of challenging the implicit universalism of familiar discourse, and hence exposing the presumptions in it that marginalise and displace other ways of seeing the political world. These chapters are of course refracted through translation and smoothed by the editorial hand (a light one here). But the cultural multiplicity and intellectual diversity of the contributions below should challenge an Anglophone scholarly community that is perhaps too accustomed to talking just to itself, or presuming that it is entitled to talk over the heads of others.

Rather than review the papers for the reader in the somewhat redundant way that editorial introductions often attempt, we have chosen to develop what we see as the purpose behind the collection, and to recount the achievements within it. This takes the form of an extended argument concerning new interpretive methodologies. The chapters in this book are then related to our framework, and to each other, as they illustrate the themes that we take up. In the text below, all references are to chapters in this book, citing the author by surname.

INTERPRETATION

Broadly, interpretive methodologies remind practitioners that social science is conducted through the medium of language, and that language is not a transparent 'window' on 'fact'. Neither quantitative formulations nor redefinitions in 'value-neutral' terms allow political science or conventional narrative studies of politics to become extra-discursive. For those reasons, political science requires techniques of analysis developed from advances in semiotics and linguistics.

A number of different though related developments in methodological thinking are present in this work: hermeneutic theories of truth and explanation, discourse theories of language and symbolic representation, the 'linguistic and rhetorical turn' in post-Wittgensteinian philosophy, deconstruction in conceptual analysis, anti-foundational perspectives on knowledge, and contextualism in linguistic analysis.

A particular unifying feature of this collection is the focus on developing an interpretive methodology and applying it to a substantive problem in politics. Thus there are no purely methodological papers, nor methodologically uninformed presentations of research. The variety of political events and issues discussed is indicative of recent trends in 'rethinking the political'. The aim is to move enquiry towards multidisciplinary methods and to research areas that will reach a wider audience. Thus in choosing these papers the editors have striven to show how far the boundaries of 'what is political' are already moving within the discipline itself.

Research purpose and the researcher–subject relationship are continuing themes of these essays, as this is again an element of social scientific method that is underdeveloped in political science. Moreover it is one that is best discussed in the context of actual research on substantive issues. The notion of what constitutes a research source is deliberately extended in this collection in unusual ways, including autobiographical interviewing (Hyvärinen), political science participation studies as political texts (Keränen), national anthems and other symbolic constructions of community and nationhood (Bleicher, Sondermann), travelling and travel writing (Palonen), media images and texts as a political nexus of public participation (Bresnihan, Carver), simulations and video games as both objects of study and methods for study in international politics (Der Derian), and popular writing in social science as a political strategy (Mottier).

Political scientists and other students of politics could – and should – profit from new strategies and techniques in interpretation. The attempt to politicise a new group of themes would have been quite unintelligible just a few decades ago. Themes were then either political or not, and there was no active movement for changing the boundaries. 'Reading' politically is therefore a new movement with academic and political implications, and all papers in this collection share in this perspective.

READING

During the last few decades, reading has become the root metaphor for many political, cultural and social scientific activities. We read images, 'body language', films, architecture, anything that has meaning. Even in sport, particularly in markedly tactical games like football, players have to read the play of the opposing team. This vision of the social and political world as something game-like yet awaiting an interpretive reading by participants and spectators is not, of course, wholly new in the 1990s. It owes a good deal to the mature Wittgenstein and his 'language games' – and to a number of other scholars. But these methods were newly introduced into political studies in the 1980s, and this collection aims to consolidate the achievements.

However, it is quite beyond the intentions and resources of the editors to review in detail the linkage between the 'linguistic turn' in philosophy and reading as a methodology in the social sciences. What we undertake is rather to show some of what lies behind the present interest in reading, and particularly in reading politically. We cannot uncover a singular origin for, nor a single trajectory of, reading, but rather a plethora of different beginnings and approaches, more or less entangled. This is, of course, a very political tangle of traditions, institutions, personal interests and judgements.

But why reading? This is a truly general term, something like intellectual breathing. What could be a more natural activity for researchers than reading? How does reading become a distinctive metaphor, and signify something non-trivial?

What is required to make sense of this metaphor is the conviction that words and tropes, sentences and narratives are not what they seem to be. There are certain requirements for political reading. However sound it is to distinguish textual 'surface' from underlying 'deep' structures, it is also necessary to consider the surface text sensitively enough. Political reading does not presuppose mere dissociation or deconstruction. The task is to discover our different political potentialities, and a strict method may lead too hastily to a theoretical world 'behind' or 'under' the text.

Increasing sensitivity to textual surface has been one of the common objectives of the newer strategies of reading. Closely related to this is an emerging focus on the construction, and self-construction, of the individual through language. When a conception of language as a simple tool was trenchantly criticised, the first result was often its structuralist extreme: language and discourses were seen as primary agents of social dramas, neatly condensed in the slogan 'we do not speak language, language speaks us'. Similarly, the followers of Foucault-the-archaeologist made 'discourse' into an active subject, capable of acting like a political agent. But it is now generally accepted that only humans act, individually or in groups, and so act politically.

As a resource, language is peculiar. Our acts almost always have unintended consequences, and speech acts are no exception. A language user is never in a position to master and control all of the aspects and potential consequences of conceptual or rhetorical devices. On the contrary, most language usage is spontaneous enough to justify the description 'quasi-automatic'. For instance, we acquire and we create our political horizons – where to situate our intentional acts, hopes and struggles – only by means of basic concepts of politics, and when we act we reinscribe those horizons in ourselves and others.

THE SELF

Problems with 'language use' do not cease here. It is more than evident that the 'language user' is a construct of language usage, that is, created in discourse. Thus we can no longer leave the 'users' aside, because they themselves are an important result of linguistic practice itself. The self is not a pre-linguistic given. The political and existential self is therefore continuously constructed by means of narrative and rhetoric (Carver). In particular, in order to be able to change the course of our lives, we seem to need a corresponding rhetoric of the 'divided self' (Hyvärinen). The 'production of the self' may well be a very conscious project. This is the case with the 'sound-bytes' and memoirs of politicians, who try to answer questions like 'what should the self of a competent politician look like?', 'which kind of slogans and recollections bolster that kind of image best?'

The relation between language and the speaker is no longer external. This is one of the key ideas of the constructionist orientation to language and reading. It has long been a common notion that individual agents, such as persons, political parties or social movements, construct realities of their own. Constructionism is now not directed towards the individual or particular mode of cognition but rather towards the very construction of the social world itself in speech and language. Accordingly, we should study how different social constructions – like personal identity (Carver, Hyvärinen), the nation (Palonen, Sondermann), intellectual and political artefacts like the EC (Bleicher) and political science (Keränen), sexuality (Mottier), or leaders and enemies (Bresnihan, Der Derian) – are produced in language usage. Moreover, much of our studies of 'facts', such as voter apathy or defence policy, or 'events', such as elections or political decision-making, are really studies of the effects of these constructions.

POLITICS

Reading politicians themselves puts the focus on a political problem. It is not difficult to employ the sophisticated methods of semiotics, hermeneutics, rhetoric or discourse analysis in a way that makes politicians seem naive. But this attitude underestimates politicians and their capacity to invent new linguistic resources. Rather we should take politicians seriously. Their speech and 'appearances' or image are not to be judged solely in terms of historical or societal categories, or universalistic normative criteria. The potential for creativity in politics appears in view once we focus on rhetoric. And here we also encounter a civic capacity for reading politically: new groups, from feminists to nationalists, read new areas of life as political. Who is a politician is itself an open question.

To reformulate the boundaries of political thinking, we should not reverse but reshape certain dichotomies. Both voluntarism and determinism share the basic conception that action is outwardly determined, either out of will or out of deterministic categories (e.g. class, culture, nationality). Everything that is incidental, unpredictable or uncontrollable is in this context irrelevant and marginalised. This suggests some directions for political reading.

When the direction of deconstructive reading is from top to bottom, the reading is accordingly 'politicalising'. Political reading may, therefore, deconstruct law-like generalisations and expose the contingent potentialities present in texts. Similarly, a political reading would deconstruct homogenising views like 'West' and 'East' or 'non-Western' or 'Third World'. Thus conflict and plurality in interpretations, rather than a tendency to stereotypes, should prevail.

This approach to 'political' and 'political reading' recognises that politics is not natural, determined or homogeneously present in 'institutions of power'. Instead, an interpretive method understands politics historically, as a specific potentiality. Reading politically, in this context, is also a political act, maintaining and generating this potentiality. It is incompatible with this perspective of contingent, plural and conflictual politics to read so as to find 'underlying regularities' beneath 'surface traces'. This would be reading texts from below to above; that is, unpolitically. This does not mean, however, that we advocate moving away from further sophisticated techniques for reading – quite the contrary. Plurality is the key word, even here.

Reading politically is not the same as applying a method, and it necessarily requires craft and imagination. Both of these, again, require acquaintance with diverse tools for interpretation and with various interpretations of the political. This is what the reader will find in the chapters that follow.

2 Identity and narrative in prime-time politics
The Hill–Thomas hearings

Terrell Carver

I think it's very interesting to listen to her because as I saw her there, she said it's a matter of interpretation . . . [']A long time ago this happened. I didn't do anything about it.['] . . . I don't say that it didn't happen but I'm convinced that there's another side to this story that says that it did not happen, at least in this manner, as this lady has put forward.

Q[UESTION] Senator, you're making a decision here based on accepting his credibility over her credibility.

A[NSWER] That's my job, yes, ma'am.

(New York Times, 8 October 1991)

. . . every 15 minutes there was a new theory . . .

Anita Hill (New York Times, 15 October 1991)

Clarence Thomas was the black, Republican nominee for Associate Justice of the US Supreme Court, filling a seat vacated by the first black man to hold that office. Anita Hill was a black, Republican law professor whose allegations suddenly disrupted the orderly process of confirmation. She claimed that Thomas had sexually harassed her when they had both worked at the Equal Employment Opportunities Commission, the federal agency responsible for implementing directives on sexual harassment. The Democrat majority on the Senate Judiciary Committee assigned to review Thomas was accused by Hill of not taking her allegations seriously because the committee was entirely male; the sole female Republican Senator steadfastly supported Thomas. The episode attracted vast media and public interest, and was widely regarded at the time as of historic importance in US politics. It still is.

I have taken the *New York Times* account of the Hill–Thomas hearings of 1991 in the Judiciary Committee of the US Senate as a text for interpretive analysis. This analysis dissolves traditional distinctions between participants, spectators and researchers in a politically interesting and radically democratic way. My hypotheses in this study were threefold: first, that sexual, racial and class politics interacted in a new manner in the US; second, that narrative analysis would reveal interesting sub-texts, of which I found two – Manichaean constructions in *Times* journalism and the persistent assumption that credibility follows from consistency; and third, I hypothesised that symbols and simulacra would become analytically relevant.

However, my major finding was not hypothesised at the outset. It is that interpretive methodology was self-consciously and strategically employed by participants themselves. I suggest that this 'narrative multiplication', which I describe in detail, was responsible for the Thomas victory in the Senate vote. In conclusion I speculate on what this may mean for politics in the future, and I argue for a 'science fiction of politics' to replace 'political science'.

INTERPRETATION

Americans often say, 'It's a matter of interpretation.' Well, yes it is, but it is only recently that this insight has burst upon the social sciences, in what is known as the interpretive or linguistic 'turn'. This is a 'turn' in methodology, and of necessity in basic assumptions. Specifically it encompasses the claim that understanding arises out of textual interpretation, and that mechanistic or law-like 'explanations' of human 'behaviour' based on the supposed protocols of natural science are bogus.

'Behaviour' itself is invariably textualised when it is studied; 'data sets' are actually texts and have been shown to be embedded in broader narratives (Giddens 1982, 1987; for specific applications see, for example, Ball 1987 on political science, Lavoie 1990 on economics, and Shanks and Tilly 1987 on archaeology). Objects of interpretation that can be 'read' as texts have successively expanded to include artefacts such as films or other images and objects such as the human body or fossils (Boyne and Rattansi 1990; Haraway 1991). Further, deconstructionist or postmodern writers have successfully made problematic the notions of 'author' and 'reader' that interpretation requires (Murphy 1989; Ryan 1988). Moreover illocutionary philosophies of language have evolved theories of 'performative utterance' that locate 'understanding' in a context of motivations and goals; 'we understand differently when we understand at all' (Gadamer, quoted in Lavoie 1990: 2). 'Understanding' takes place in a political context and is inevitably *for* some purpose or purposes, or functions as if it had such a purpose, and is inevitably interpreted within a purposive framework (Tully 1988). Of necessity this perspective extends to the interpreter or researcher, and I shall offer my own view of the utility of the present discussion at its close.

I have taken as my text the account of the Hill–Thomas hearings presented by the *New York Times* (hereafter *NYT*), 7–20 October 1991. The *NYT* is a newspaper of record with exceptionally full coverage, much verbatim material, a range of very well-informed reporting, and far more reliability and insight than most journalism. Alternative or further studies could include videotapes from the various national networks that carried the hearings, radio tapes or transcripts of coverage, and other newspaper and journal accounts (I have also made use of the *Washington Post* weekly edition, the *New York Review of Books* and *Judicature*).

The amount of text or text-like materials that tell us about this kind of event expands towards the infinite, especially if polling or interviewing is considered. The *NYT* includes a good deal of this type of material, as reporters were dispatched to a number of 'unlikely' places to relate what 'ordinary Americans' were thinking. The notion that the Hill–Thomas hearings were an 'event' or 'series of events' thus becomes problematic, as there are in a sense as many 'events' as there are individuals who took some view about the 'participants' and what they said. Because what 'participants' said was politically charged all along, the circle of actual participants widened to include those in the various 'publics' who might somehow register a reaction, most notably through the opinion polls, Congressional mail and telephone calls, and ultimately votes.

Thus there is no neat way to 'frame' participants or narrative. The presumed distinctions between participants, spectators and commentators swiftly dissolve into the conversational production of text: the typical *NYT* reporter filed a story containing first-hand observation, quotation from major figures, comments from associates and bystanders, telephone interview and opinion poll information, and a good-sized dollop of personal interpretive technique ranging from overtly radical feminism (Maureen Dowd) to traditional 'veteran' reporting (R.W. Apple).

Everyone had their own Hill–Thomas hearings. But not all accounts are equally interesting, nor is there any one 'authoritative' version. The *NYT* is an interesting palimpsest to look at because it draws on so many sources and commands a loyal but critical audience. As an interlocutor for persuasive and transformative 'conversation' in politics, it is better than most.

There can be little doubt that the hearings will be memorialised by political and cultural historians as a significant event. The US Senate put itself through a uniquely contorted bout of self-criticism and self-defence. The TV audiences were enormous, and other media coverage was extensive. Parallels with historic events were swiftly established, notably the McCarthy hearings of the early 1950s. And most importantly, the language was lurid and the drama intense. This was raunchy talk direct from the US Capitol; it was courtroom drama with contradictory witnesses; it was sex, lies and daytime TV.

HYPOTHESES

My hypotheses in doing this study were as follows. First, I presumed that sexual, racial and partisan politics were made to interact in a new way. To that hypothesis I added the view, derived from the *NYT*, that class was also an issue, as both Hill and Thomas presented themselves as, and were viewed as, elite professional lawyers (both were graduates of Yale Law School), and therefore shared, or apparently shared, anti-sexist assumptions and equal opportunities rhetoric that working-class Americans, when interviewed, generally did not.

Second, I hypothesised that narrative analysis of analogy and metaphor would reveal a set of interesting sub-texts. I presumed that Hill's calm references to 'information' and 'integrity', and Thomas's counter-allegation that he was the 'victim of a high-tech lynching' would be typical of presentational strategies adopted by any and all who could get media coverage. This could of course extend to dress, deportment, entourage and general considerations of 'image-making'.

I was struck by two sub-texts in particular. One was the persistent construction of 'stories' by various *NYT* reporters around Manichaean dualisms and dramatic contradictions: the prim farm girl versus the cut-throat world of Washington careers; hallowed halls of Congress versus raunchy language and locker-room talk; a full Senate vote as a verdict on who was lying; reputations definitively on the line.

This sports-page journalism seemed surprisingly old-fashioned after *Hill Street Blues*, the American television series of the early 1980s that left viewers with loose ends, story-lines that never finished and a general feeling of real-life anarchy. Thomas will be for-ever scrutinised on the bench and off it, in the light of his histrionic claims of ignorance, innocence and integrity. Hill will continue to command respect as the woman who came forward courageously to challenge the male power structure. What happened to her will be interpreted as further reason for women to win public office. The interpretation of political events is not as neatly dichotomous as the *NYT* narrative suggested.

The other sub-text was the overwhelming persistence of consis-tency as the sole and ultimate test of credibility, when, as the FBI put it, the case was of the 'he said, she said' variety (note the sexual transposition). Throughout the *NYT* narrative the supposition that the truthful individual is consistent, not just in stating and defend-ing a truth, but in all aspects of behaviour alleged to be relevant, reigned supreme. Hill suffered particularly for her decision to move to another federal agency in Washington after the alleged harass-ment, and therefore to work with Thomas again. Thomas distin-guished himself at the hearings overall by claiming ludicrous blanks in his experience or recollections of it – this was known as the 'stealth strategy' (Melone *et al.* 1992), and refusing to comment on what he considered to be private. Inconsistency in 'character' meant ruin and madness in the *NYT*, whereas memory lapses and categori-cal evasions did not seem to matter.

But do any of us know ourselves sufficiently well to be able to find out whether the 'self' that we presume must be 'in there' is con-sistent or not? At the end of the debate and after the vote the *NYT* did report some thoughtful musing on whether any nominee could stand up to such scrutiny of 'character', although the presumed ground for scepticism was much more probably the existence of original sin than the non-existence of the continuous self (Carrithers *et al.* 1985; Elster 1986).

How one constructs a narrative in the present about the past was also bound to be an analytically interesting issue: the terms and assumptions of the present are not those of the past, and those who judge competing accounts in the present are, or ought to be, in a quandary. Do they assess the seriousness of the situation according to the standards and circumstances of the past – and if so, whose? Or do they assess past events, recounted in a narrative of the pre-sent, according to standards and circumstances that obtain at the moment – and if so, whose? Is there a way of narrating the past in its own terms? Or does any account of the past, given in the pre-sent, read the present into the past by definition?

This raises the possibility that people of the present and people of the past are necessarily different, and living in different worlds. Interestingly, the 'women's eyes/men's eyes' issue also arose, and further complicated the situation. Perhaps the committee was simply in no position to judge Hill's narrative as they could not or would not understand it; perhaps the Senate itself, which was 98 per cent male, would be in a similar position when the nomination came to the floor for a vote.

Third, I hypothesised that symbols and simulacra would become analytically relevant (Baudrillard 1988). Hill and Thomas were said by the *NYT* to have become symbolic: of the new feminist politics, of abused black women, of brave and lonely private individuals who confront the horrors of partisan mud-slinging, of the advancement of black people into the highest offices of the land, of highly paid black professionals who adopt the conservative values of the white elite, of careerism in party politics and negative campaigning.

As the hearings progressed, Hill and Thomas became inscriptions of these ideas: Hill was thirteenth in an Oklahoma farm family and introduced numerous relations to the committee, testifying in simple verbatim terms; Thomas was the man of dignity, pushed beyond endurance, forced to speak out and earnestly preferring 'the assassin's bullet' to his ordeal. In a sense they were 'copies without originals', as they had no models of themselves previously in those roles to copy; nor were they copying in exact terms anyone else, real or fictional, who had been in some similar situation. They became characters in a spontaneously generated theatrical event, as it was obvious that they had an audience to play to, and to play to an audience they needed and used a vocabulary of signs and signals surrounding themselves and emerging from themselves in multiple ways. They were neither wholly scripted nor completely unstudied; they improvised and were never short of advice, on which point the *NYT* was, as ever, newsily thorough (*NYT* 15 October 1991). When Hill and Thomas became public, politicised figures their personae necessarily changed, and their own comments revealed that they knew this to be the case. In a sense they became different people.

FINDINGS

I am, however, pleased to report that the major finding of my research was not hypothesised in advance but was in fact a complete surprise. Against expectation, I discovered that interpretive methodology was self-consciously and sophisticatedly employed by participants in the *NYT* narrative; that it was perceived as essential to participant strategies; and that the winning strategy – Thomas's – was successful, so it seems to me, precisely because it multiplied narratives, different narratives about Hill.

Thomas and his supporters (some of whom were women) employed inconsistent and contradictory narratives about Hill as a present personality, whereas Hill and her supporters had but one narrative about Thomas, and that was set in the past. Moreover she had but one narrative about herself, which she and her supporters were unable to defend successfully against counter-attack. Thomas had a non-narrative about himself and was allowed to get away with it; he lashed out in the present and was not pushed on the past, virtually all of it having become blandly 'private'. Hill, by contrast, had pushed 'private' behaviour relating to herself into the public realm, and was sternly policed for doing so.

I am not claiming that participants in the *NYT* narrative (and I emphasise that other sources would provide overlapping and corroborative accounts) employed interpretive methodologies *as methodologies*, the way they are employed here; rather they hit upon political strategies that were self-consciously interpretive. This is in a sense an instance of 'negative campaigning', which is nothing new in practice or theory. But some of the participants in the *NYT* narrative – the Thomas group – were unusually good at it. Of course, we cannot know exactly why the Senate votes fell as they did, and my conclusion that a strategy of 'narrative multiplication' was crucial is itself speculation – as intentional explanations always are, even when given by the agent in question. But I think it is highly plausible.

Having discussed these findings, I shall conclude by generalising from this study to some speculative but minatory remarks about the future, and to a sketchy but critical reconceptualisation of political science.

NARRATIVE

By the time Hill and Thomas reached the committee room, media exposure, as recounted in the *NYT*, had effectively set the stage: the hearings would be a courtroom drama *and* a TV sitcom, two genres to which the presumed mass audience could respond. Committee hearings are, at most, quasi-judicial and lack a presiding judge; effectively all participants are partisan and can behave in a relatively informal manner. Jokes, anecdotes and cosiness abounded, as did flat contradiction, mixtures of counter-claim and question, and a general sense of improvisation in the absence of clear rules and precedents. It could have been scripted, it was taped and transcripted, and it will doubtless be dramatically reconstructed on television and in the movies. Yet the dignity of the chambers, the sense of high office and responsibility, and the general feeling of a trial – albeit by ordeal – made the televised venue a courtroom in which spectators could play at being jurors, evaluating evidence and judging credibility. Narrative strategies played to both genres, creating flashback tales and novelistic characterisations. Actual trials, courtroom drama and TV sitcoms are no great distance from each other anyway; each borrows elements from the other. There is a circle of referential narrative out of which individuals, whatever their role – jurors, actors, spectators – come to the interpretive 'understandings' that they do, and the discursive strategies that they employ.

Thomas and his supporters on the committee and elsewhere hit back at Hill to save his nomination. They did this by multiplying their portrayals of her 'character' in order to impugn her 'credibility', namely 'someone like that could not have been telling the truth'. From that it was supposed to follow that Thomas was never guilty of sexual harassment and gross hypocrisy, and that therefore he was qualified to be Associate Justice of the Supreme Court. Thoughtful writers in the legal and jurisprudential community had already written, and still maintain, that he was distinctly unqualified for such a professional elevation and that his judicial record and legal abilities were never properly scrutinised (Dworkin 1991).

Thomas and his supporters, in person and by affidavit, portrayed Hill as a hard-minded, determinedly rational careerist who could never have been so innocently vulnerable a victim of sexual harassment. They also suggested that she was the victim of erotomania, a syndrome of obsessive and inexplicable sexual attraction undeterred by rebuff. She was supposedly given to fantasies and zombie-like behaviour, even schizophrenia, according to some testimony and comment. She was also said to have stolen fictions from popular books like *The Exorcist* and to have pilfered facts from obscure legal cases. When she passed a polygraph test, this was interpreted as further proof that her 'flat-out perjury' was so comprehensive that she believed the lies herself. Possibly she was vindictive and attention-seeking, not the reserved, religious and deeply private person she claimed to be. Moreover her use of consultants and media advisers was described as slick and calculating, and her motivation for coming forward could only have been political. She was said to be the tool of special-interest groups with narrow agendas, stopping at nothing in order to achieve some minority political goal. She was even portrayed as a 'Joker' figure, the character in the *Batman* film, garishly made up but grotesquely deformed, grinning insanely at destructive pranks, and glorying in the agony of victims (*NYT*, 14, 15 October 1991).

No one could have been all these things at once, and indeed no one added them up in order to evaluate their credibility, consistency and plausibility. Piecemeal denial played into the strategy. As Hill said, every fifteen minutes there was a new theory. One of the crucial elements in her defeat was her surprise at this, and another was the failure of her supporters on the committee to put Thomas through anything similar. After the Senate voted 52:48 to confirm Thomas, the Democrats were derided in the press as political wimps and closet chauvinists for failing to round on Thomas with defamatory characterisations. As Machiavelli has noted, the scrupulous fall victim to the wicked (*Discourses* II.2, 1970b).

Had the Hill camp seen the narrative assault for what it was, they could have identified it before the battle was lost and at least had a choice concerning their scruples and tactics. Possibly they should not have behaved differently, but possibly exposure of the tactics of the opposition would have vitiated some of its strength. As it was, Thomas successfully claimed that he was the victim of what can only be described as 'reputation rape'. This has the disturbing implication that he successfully played the 'Tootsie' card: men are better at being women than women are – one widely endorsed reading of the Dustin Hoffman film.

Thinking speculatively about the future, I would suggest that the proliferation of modern media coverage makes it likely that 'narrative multiplication' will become increasingly common, and that its use will be essentially negative. Against background assumptions that probity is consistency, and that any and all allegations go 'on the record' and accumulate, the dominant strategy will become the multiple smear.

POWER

New interpretive methodologies have revealed that 'political science' is a fiction; what we need instead is a 'science fiction' of politics. Fictions are what 'authors' tell us; truths are fictions that *we* tell ourselves repeatedly; they are truthful because they work – one way or another. Thomas won by invoking multiple 'truths' that took hold precisely because they were such good fictions.

In politics the past is a poor guide to the present, and the 'scientific prediction' of 'the future' derived from supposed 'law-like regularities' in past 'behaviour' is a notoriously bad way to pursue any understanding at all. My ears are still burning from having heard a well-known professor of political science jokily admit that no political scientists had predicted the fall of the Berlin Wall. Amazingly he did not seem to think that this posed any problems for the practice of 'political science'. Well, I do.

The Hill team would have done well to have read *Advise and Consent* (Drury 1959), the political novel in which scandalous allegations of communism and homosexuality emerge in and around fictional confirmation hearings, and to have developed a strategy that responded creatively to the undoubted power of the smear. This is narrative power – it is quantitative and cumulative – and there were plenty of ways to attack Thomas without stooping to quite the same level of bizarrerie. Rather than employ 'political scientists' to 'predict the outcome', based on generalisations from past 'behaviour' among the Senators, the Hill team should have turned to a 'science fiction' of politics – 'science' because it is strategically purposive rather than merely entertaining, and 'fiction' because practitioners would turn on a novelist's imagination to the principals and their situation, writing up speculative scenarios. For those scenarios strategies could be developed; indeed opponents could be pushed into narrative characterisations that they did not like very much. That is what happened to Hill.

The Thomas supporters offered plenty of hostages to fortune. He was said to have been a devotee of pornographic films while at Yale University, and his character witnesses pursued an interesting line: they argued that Hill was not generally credible because she had professional and sexual ambitions that were just as basely meretricious as . . . their own! The Thomas camp churned out narratives from the docudrama, the TV soap and the mini-series; the Hill team stuck repetitiously to integrity, understatement and good taste. Even that was undermined by snide references to certain well-exposed failings – Senator Kennedy and the 'bridge up in Massachusetts' was the most telling instance (*NYT*, 15 October 1991).

The Hill team followed academic values, the values of scholarly distance and unemotional veracity. But this presentation did not 'play in Peoria' where most Senatorial minds are, and must be, owing to the various 'publics' that they feel they have to satisfy. Some of the 'ordinary' interviewees of the *NYT* were women who thought that Hill should have dealt with whatever 'problem' there was herself, just as they had or would, or so they said (*NYT*, 15 October 1991).

Had Hill been more forthcoming in her self-characterisations, she could possibly have tipped the scales. Narrative models for the strong but vulnerable, ambitious but principled, feminine yet successful woman are thin on the ground. If there were more feminist novelists and feminist life Hill would have had a better chance, as she could have appealed to powerful narratives to support her 'credibility'.

Lives are lived fictions, some borrowed and others invented; it is this self-created and collectively acted process that creates what should be of most interest to 'political scientists'. If there are law-like regularities in human behaviour, they are not of much political interest, and if the supposition of such regularities is invoked to divert attention from the undoubted indeterminacy of human affairs, then 'political scientists' are self-deluding fools. If nothing else in 'social science' there is always the possibility of the self-fulfilling or self-negating prophecy.

'Political science' cannot succeed unless it is novelised as a 'science fiction of politics'. Fiction is a lot less strange than life; the 'science fiction of politics' will have to work hard to keep up. And we will have to consider carefully what this 'science' is for in political terms.

3 Rhetoric and conversion in student politics
Looking backward

Matti Hyvärinen

Life history is seldom taken seriously in political studies. Mainstream political scientists have generally employed interview materials as mere compilations of statements, presumed to be 'facts'. Scholars inspired by postmodernist orientations have been reluctant to employ the confessional mode, as it is individualised and 'authorial'. In contrast to this apparent unanimity on the peripheral role of life history in political studies, I argue in this chapter that reading and analysing life stories should be much more central.

First, political action always includes a revelatory aspect, confessional or not, which establishes an intimate relationship between the action and the stories told by the actors. The well-known 'character issue' in politics, for example, concerns stories told about political actors. Second, I argue that political selves and identities are routinely constituted in a narrative way. Formation and transformation of identities can be located and depicted in the study of autobiographies and life stories. There is no reason whatsoever to marginalise a biographical approach within political science.

IDENTITY, CONTINUITY AND COHERENCE

In this chapter, I consider the problem of identity formation in terms of continuity and coherence. Political actors are usually presumed to present their lives and identities as a continuity. Stories that manifest a radical outward turn or rupture are the severest test of coherence. My main illustration here is the story of a female Finnish student activist from the movement of the 1970s.

In the early 1970s, Anu Rantanen, like so many of her fellow students, joined the pro-Soviet Marxist–Leninist Socialist Student Union (SOL), and soon became a member of the Finnish

Communist Party as well. In terms of the political expectations of the cold war era, this move should have been a highly radical political turn, or even conversion. In June 1989, when interviewed, she had left the Marxist project and its organisations far behind her, and had created a new and successful career as a middle-class professional. What was the character of the self and of her identity under these circumstances, given the changes involved?

Methodologically, my key concern will be the politics of reading. This methodology implies that interviews are not the reservoirs of fact that mainstream or 'realist' political scientists suppose they are. The 'facts' are not 'out there', waiting for the researcher. Rather they are created in a double interaction: first, in the personal interaction between the interviewer and the interviewee (Mishler 1986); and second, in an even more radical way, in the process through which the reader interprets the text. Because I have discussed my interviewing strategy elsewhere (Hyvärinen 1992), I will now focus on the second kind of interaction.

The term 'politics of reading' refers to the necessarily active and potent role that reading plays in political life. Literary theorists of autobiography have elaborated this point in a very helpful way. During the last fifteen years, several feminist critics have attacked the concept of the autonomous and individualised self which, in the 1960s, was supposed to be the final outcome of any autobiographical project. Women, so the argument goes, are much more relational than the male individual, which was supposedly the abstract norm (Mason 1980; Friedman 1988). Nancy K. Miller (1994) has radicalised this criticism by insisting that relationality between individuals may also be understood as a way of reading. The wholly autonomous individual was not exclusively a product of male writers; male readers and male theorists were needed as well. Her critical test was to show how the classical conversion narrative of St Augustine (1961) can be better understood relationally as a process of reconciliation with his mother Monica.

However, my objectives in this chapter are much more limited. My views will evolve as a succession of separate readings. For my research, I conducted interviews with thirty-six former student activists, asking for an autobiography. Nevertheless, my interpretative work begins here with the story of Anu Rantanen (the name is fictional). Her life story illustrates the transformation of my own concepts, expectations and methodological apparatus (Hyvärinen 1994). Using this example, I demonstrate how the expectations and prejudices of the researcher guide an interpretation. Correspondingly, I try to show how a hidden normativity in descriptive concepts such as 'thickness' (developed by Denzin) can be misleading. Finally, I make a strong case for changing the concepts through which successive interpretations are constructed by a single interpreter. To illustrate this argument, I focus on the concept of 'conversion story'.

I conducted the interviews between October 1987 and January 1990. For some of the narrators, the contemporary breakdown of East European socialism was a major incentive to reflect on their life stories, but most of them had rejected Marxism–Leninism and the Communist Party years before. Each interview lasted from two to three hours and resulted in fifty to seventy pages of transcribed text. The easiest way to proceed from transcription to interpretation might have been to choose a traditional realistic or even journalistic mode of reading, and to tell the story of the Finnish student movement as it unfolded. This would involve picking up picturesque quotations from well-known leaders and writing with profound empathy of the hopes and sufferings that these particular activists experienced.

Why not be content with this solution, so beautifully exemplified by Ronald Fraser (1988) and his co-authors? I was not in fact persuaded that there was one movement and one story. From my nominalist point of view, social movements need to be rhetorically constituted in society. They exist if relevant actors, opponents and audiences believe in their existence. They are products of complex political and social negotiations.

Who belongs to a social movement? Which organisations should be included and which excluded? It is impossible to answer these questions adequately without substantial institutionalisation of a movement. To study 'the movement of 1968' indicates agreement on the part of the researcher that this construct exists, and, what is more problematic, it implies approval for a re-creation of this discursive figuration.

However, my aims have been much more deconstructive. I preferred collecting various stories concerned with activism in this period, precisely in order to question the one-story model, as characteristically recounted by the former leaders. Instead of interviewing only known leaders and celebrities, I tried to sensitise myself to the various hierarchical levels of the movement, including gendered strata.

The result of this reasoning was a gradual shift in my interest away from the collective movement to the narrated self and its identity. This shift necessitated a closer look at the rhetoric and narrative in the life stories. However, before I can proceed to detailed discussion, I need to consider the relationship between autobiography and political action, and to say something about the Finnish context.

AUTOBIOGRAPHY AS A POLITICAL ACT

Is there anything that can be understood as 'political' in autobiographical documents? Literary theorists have exhaustively analysed the political nature of autobiographies. One of the peculiarities that emerged from these discussions was the simultaneous appearance of outstanding autobiographies and political revolutions and upheavals (Cox 1989). St Augustine's *Confessions* coincided with the breakthrough of Christianity in the Roman world; Montaigne studied himself in the midst of civil war; and Jean-Jacques Rousseau was not merely one of the inventors of modern autobiography but a major figure in the build-up to the French Revolution.

The same sort of relationship seems to prevail between major social movements and the flow of autobiographies. The Emancipation Proclamation was preceded by an abolitionist 'literature of the slave', which attested to their human nature (Gates 1988: 52–57; Cox 1989: 3). The *Autobiography of Malcolm X* and numerous feminist autobiographies have accompanied major social movements since the 1960s. These overt representations of political lives allude to the more intimate and intrinsic political character of autobiographical expression.

The fundamental closeness of political views, political actions and life stories was clear to Hannah Arendt, who emphasised the *revealing* aspect of political action: 'In acting and speaking, men show who they are, reveal actively their unique personal identities and thus make their appearance in the human world' (1958: 179). Arendt does not include confessionality in her discussion of action and politics. The point of such confessions is not to reveal secret sins, in the way that St Augustine did, but rather political identity: *who* someone is. The imperfect human condition and the surge of contingency give an inevitable quality to the narrative. Because of the 'already existing web of human relationships, with its innumerable, conflicting wills and intentions . . . action almost never achieves its purpose' (Arendt 1958: 184). Purposes are not fulfilled, and the outcomes of the action tend to be irreversible. This particular state of affairs generates stories, 'the results of action and speech'. When the heroine is dead, it is time for the biographer to tell us who she was.

It is important now to contrast autobiography with biography. Both are life stories, of course, but autobiography shares with action a particular *performatory* nature. Biographies study and describe the identities of actors; autobiographies are an active performance in themselves in order to create and fulfill these identities. Elisabeth Bruss (1976) was the first to discuss autobiographies from the perspective of speech acts. Porter Abbot (1988) theorised this point further by describing autobiography as personal action. To read a text autobiographically, Abbot contends, 'is to ask of a text: How does this reveal the author?' (1988: 613).

The performance of telling one's life story now has a double meaning. The first is to compose or construct the story, instead of passively recounting the supposed life itself. Jerome Bruner (1990: 121) has aptly described the other component of the performance:

> There is something curious about autobiography. . . . [T]he larger story reveals a strong rhetorical strand, as if justifying why it was necessary (*not* causally, but morally, socially, psychologically) that the life had gone a particular way. The Self as narrator not only recounts but justifies. And the Self as protagonist is always, as it were, pointing to the future. When somebody says, as if summing up a childhood, 'I was a pretty rebellious kid', it can usually be taken as a prophecy as much as a summary.

The very first thing a life story has to accomplish is to form itself with a certain amount of coherence. '[A]utobiography properly speaking assumes the task of reconstructing the unity of life across time', as Georges Gusdorf puts it in his well-known essay (1980: 37). Taking this position does not imply any essentialist assumptions about the (in)coherence of 'real life'. Rather than debate 'essentialism' and 'real life', it is more helpful to try to identify the particular strategies and institutions of coherence which are used in actual life stories (Denzin 1989: 62).

These 'constructive' and 'justifying' aspects of life stories call for corresponding methods of analysis. In the discussion that follows, I argue for the use of rhetorical analysis for these purposes. The rhetorical study of life stories enquires into the way that stories and arguments are constructed, and into what persuasive power these stories and expressions have. As a future-oriented act, autobiography is always presented to an audience. The triangle of classical rhetorics – *ethos*, *pathos* and *logos* – elegantly covers the political character of the autobiography (Perelman and Olbrechts-Tyteca 1971; Edmondson 1984).

Now I return to my original problem of conversion, and in particular, the rhetoric of conversion. On this issue I was very impressed by the patristic tradition of autobiography, and in particular by the *Confessions* of St Augustine. The dramatic turn in these stories occurs at a conversion. Monika Wohlrab-Sahr (1992) has linked *a change in a person* to *a change of interpretative framework*, and she refers to conversion as *a paradigm shift*. Entering and leaving a communist movement apparently involves a shift of paradigm, and at least potentially a change in a person.

Charles Griffin offers a different approach to the problem of conversion as seen in his *rhetorical reading* of a conversion story. His analysis of Chuck Colson's *Born Again* dramatises spiritual conversion clearly. This successful lawyer and adviser to President Nixon found his God during the Watergate scandal, confessed his sins publicly and was sent to gaol. However, as Griffin convincingly puts it, this striking turn in Colson's life does not indicate any incoherence or rupture of his story – quite the contrary. Conversion was experienced as a decisive contest between pride and humility, the antagonistic forces in Colson's life. This rhetorical dichotomy does not only characterise the moment of conversion; it also permeates the whole story from childhood through life after conversion. The narrative is thus a syllogistic form of quasi-causality:

> Pride, the fall, humbling himself before God, striving to reform through acts of humility. This dynamic of events in Colson's narrative, with each leading progressively to the next, is a sequence that argues for the authenticity of his conversion by showing how it follows from events in his early life even as it anticipates events in his later life.
>
> (Griffin 1990: 157)

It is easy to see how decisive the rhetoric of pride and humility is in Colson's story. The experience of radical change in his life provides coherence in the story; rupture and continuity by no means appear as opposites. However, is this so only because of the religious nature of his conversion? Would it be legitimate to apply these inferences to political changes of mind? Or is it also possible to find 'non-conversional' rhetoric of the self in oral life stories?

MOVEMENT ON THE PERIPHERY

Until the 1960s Finland had a peripheral and even isolated position with regard to Western Europe. Political currents such as the New Left and the student movement in general arrived somewhat belatedly. One of the most peculiar outcomes of this delay was that the peak of activism did not appear in Finland in 1968 but rather in the early 1970s. However, this late emergence did not simply result in a delayed movement, rather it resulted in a movement evolving in a markedly different context.

Because mass student activism arrived so late in Finland, it coincided with mounting criticism elsewhere of 'anti-authoritarian' and New Left currents in the student movement. Guerrilla wars all around the Third World, the successful Tet offensive in Vietnam, the outcomes of May 1968 in Paris as well as the occupation of Czechoslovakia – all contributed to a certain conceptual and metaphorical turn in radical discussions. 'Revolution' appeared as an ever more intriguing key metaphor of the movement. Correspondingly, the younger generation adopted 'war' as a representative metaphor for politics (Burke 1945: 59–61).

But what does this change in key metaphors explain? Richard Rorty has suggested that scientific revolutions can be interpreted as 'metaphorical redescriptions' (Rorty 1989: 16). Following Donald Davidson, he also asserts that new metaphors actually 'mean nothing', and they are better understood as extra-linguistic provocations. What is most relevant here is that this metaphorical use of noises and marks 'is the sort [of thing] which makes us get busy developing a new theory' (Rorty 1989: 17). I suggest that this account of scientific revolutions may be extended to cover political changes as well.

Accordingly, I would argue that the metaphors of 'revolution' and 'politics is war' more than anything else 'made us get busy developing a new theory' (I was myself a participant in this movement). New slogans on 'revolution' in the university, education or wherever, did not originally mean anything strictly Marxist, Maoist or Marxist–Leninist. Nevertheless, these slogans posed the engendering questions: What kind of a revolution? How to make a revolution?

All this can only partly explain the final success of the pro-Soviet Marxist–Leninist student organisation Socialist Student Union (SOL), which became one of the core organisations and the most characterising force within the Finnish student movement.

The relationship between the young radicals and President Urho Kekkonen is central to understanding the student politics of this period. During his time in office (1956–81), Kekkonen promoted what was called 'friendly relationships' with the Soviet Union. This project included an extremely realistic foreign policy, steadily increasing domestic self-censorship, attempts to rewrite current history, and cynical use of foreign policy in order to foster his domestic power. All in all, this project pushed Kekkonen into conflict with a large sector of the culturally dominant middle classes.

Because of this coincidence, a relevant part of the young modernisers chose to support Kekkonen as early as the beginning of the 1960s. During the 1960s, Kekkonen was more or less openly fighting against the same older generation of conservative intellectuals as the young radicals. Consequently, the close relationship between Kekkonen and radical students was never broken, quite unlike the case of de Gaulle and the movement of 1968.

This odd relationship had a great many important consequences. In the aftermath of the occupation of Czechoslovakia – which Kekkonen condemned quite openly – the Soviet interest in controlling public discussion in Finland grew notably. Kekkonen reacted by trying to silence all public criticism of the Soviet Union. The general atmosphere was therefore highly conducive to Marxism–Leninism in its Soviet version. No one, save the relatively few Maoists, was interested in circulating anything very critical of the Soviet Union.

In this political setting, all the youth organisations – from Conservatives to Communists – were eager to manifest their 'maturity in foreign policy', a position that was redescribed with hindsight as 'Finlandisation'. In this competition to be the best of best friends, the adoption of Marxism–Leninism and a pro-Soviet policy was, of course, the final proof of being a more genuine friend than anybody else, including President Kekkonen.

Besides the President, there was also a Communist Party, which was one of the three biggest in Western Europe until the early 1970s. Thanks to the President, Communists were able to participate in the coalition government in 1966, together with Social Democrats and the Centre Party. The results of this move turned out to be seriously disappointing for the radicals who were expecting dramatic changes in power structures. The Communist Party itself split into two antagonistic currents so that a bare majority opted for the less Stalinist wing. Under the tight guidance of Soviet comrades, and regulated by their money, the party was formally held together until the mid-1980s, even though the actual state of affairs – since the late 1960s – was in fact a devastating struggle between the two factions. The more Stalinist minority faction began first to criticise and then to oppose the politics of the 'popular front' governments, in particular the incomes policy. The effect was complemented by minority rhetoric, which was full of principled talk about 'revolution' and 'Marxism–Leninism'. Ironically enough, as a minority it eventually appeared in the guise of a revitalising movement inside the bureaucratic majority faction, and not a bit as a Stalinist party of apparatchiks. Most of the student revolutionaries, including the Socialist Student Union (SOL), were therefore ready to ally themselves with this more Stalinist minority wing in the party.

The political culture of the Finnish student movement was accordingly somewhat odd because old-fashioned meetings, establishing and taking over organisations, giving resolutions and distributing leaflets, were all paradigmatic forms of politics proper. Enthusiasm in organisations was generally shared among active students, but it was nowhere as cultivated as in SOL, the organisation which had comprised five separate hierarchical levels since 1975. The decline of SOL set in about the same time as its organisation was finally complete.

It is not hard to see that the student activists may have experienced political conversions of some sort before and after their periods of activism.

ANU RANTANEN – NO CONVERSION AT ALL?

Why do I take up the story of Anu Rantanen? Not because her story was typical or even representative among my materials, nor even because of some great similarity between her interpretations and mine.

My reasons are different. The interview situation itself turned out to be somewhat problematic. During the interview Anu fell repeatedly silent. To break the silence, I had to pose more questions than I actually wanted to do, in order to get the story to run. She was clearly answering in a way that I had not anticipated. After the first questions, the interview seemed to proceed clumsily, not to say chaotically. In my research notebook I used expressions like 'taciturn, thoughtful'. But I also felt that the interview was particularly intense.

The story apparently differed significantly from the narratives of well-known leaders, and also from my own. Furthermore, one of the issues for me was how to construct coherence in a life story. Why not begin with a story that is not characterised by any obvious coherence, continuity and chronology?

I faced a similar problem with the concreteness of the interview. Norman K. Denzin (1989: 93–4) has evaluated biographical documents in terms of 'thick' or 'thin' descriptions. 'Thick' descriptions are highly valued:

> Biographical, situational thick descriptions re-create the sights, sounds, and feelings of persons and places. They permit entry into situations of experience . . . . This description of a situation locates a person in it . . . . A thick relational description brings a relationship alive.

From this normative perspective the Rantanen interview was disappointing. The story was rather thin, abstract and generalising, in contrast to Denzin's 'thickness'. This was a reason to evaluate the interview as a failure, and even to drop it from the final version of my report. However, I was determined to see the matter the other way round: to evaluate the norm of 'thickness' in terms of my material.

The first task was to ask myself, why did the story appear chaotic in my first reading? There are at least three possible reasons for this. Perhaps Anu was a chaotic narrator. On the other hand, it may have been a problem of discursive style and strategy which I had not previously recognised. Finally, there was the least flattering alternative, that the problem resides in the situation and interaction of the interview itself.

To prompt a political life story, I generally posed the question: 'How did you get interested in politics and become a Leftist, then a member of SOL?' Through this generality, I tried to leave both the point of departure and composition of the story open. Anu's answer runs: 'of course, one could say now . . . that why not . . . . That it wasn't perhaps . . . a very exceptional solution in that situation.'

Anu began by answering a 'how' question with 'why'. She related herself to others and denied her own special individuality. Next, she moved on to herself and pointed out that the direction of her political solution 'was, perhaps, one way or another clear to me'.

Joining the movement appears, then, to be something very natural. This naturalising rhetoric already excludes a great deal of the usual drama of the solution. Her next comment was as illuminating: 'perhaps one should discuss in several ways why one went . . . along'.

Here, the narrator reveals her methodology of looking for reasons: one must think them over from different points of view. Instead of simply telling the story of the protagonist, herself, she was systematically analysing the reasons for joining SOL. In fact, she answered several questions with similar systematic accounts.

Anu actively denied an alternative account: that she had joined SOL only because of social contacts. She herself decided to enter meetings and gatherings where new friendship relations were established. Finally, a surprising counter-argument surfaced: what kind of alternatives were there to joining SOL?

Instead of disclosing a dramatic and personal conversion, Anu told of a very natural, slow and piecemeal development close to a mere matter of course. Her personal change was embedded in that of her generation: 'perhaps there [in SOL] . . . the feeling, these feelings and the way of experiencing . . . were somewhat parallel [with those of mine]'.

The basic argument that Anu gives for joining SOL is *generational*, not personal. Her way of experiencing and feeling the world in general, and the political gatherings of left-wing politics in particular, was parallel with the experiences of her fellow students. Here, as in many other occasions, the word 'perhaps' recurred several times. This can be interpreted as signifying that Anu did not see her past as a finished product. During the discussion, her memory made repeated movements from the present to the past, but without finding one overarching story. The past was filled with possibilities; it was still a problematic past.

The style that Anu chose was that of analytical reasoning. Charlotte Linde (1993: 67–94) makes an important distinction between 'narrative' and 'explanation' as discursive units. I had expected a narrative of the events that led Anu to join SOL. Against my expectations, she answered by offering explanations instead of narratives. I also read the interview under this presupposition and wondered at the repeated leaps of time, 'the breaks of the story', and concluded by suspecting that her story was chaotic. Expectations on the part of the reader, therefore, can result in grave misunderstandings unless the style of discourse itself is analysed. Explanations are used, Linde says, when the recounted experiences have been problematic.

How did Anu join SOL, after all? This story was actually told in some twenty lines. It was a year of observing and then 'seeking her way to the gangs'. Instead of epiphanies, Anu presents plain statements: 'One met some people and then went on to join the organisation with them.'

Besides the rhetoric of 'perhaps', she repeatedly employed certain interesting stylistic vehicles. How and why did she use the third person, speaking about 'one' as an agent? It is not precisely a method of denying her own responsibility or initiative, because she used direct speech most of the time. The third person seems to indicate memory moving back and trying to recollect dubious and problematic pictures from the past. In particular, the experiences related to her most serious involvement seem to hide behind an insuperable barrier. They simply cannot be recalled as 'thick', colourful experiences.

The story about leaving the movement was a bit 'thicker', although it was hard to find any dramatic turning point: 'It was about '74–'75 when a certain feeling of being fed up appeared . . . and one gradually became lazier and lazier.'

This satiety is expressed in the story through recurring changes of moods: *at first* high spirits prevailed in the gatherings, *then* they became repetitive. While the story-line itself did not display radical turns, it is revealing to find this sharp dichotomy between contrasting moods. These moods divide 'the time before' from 'the time after' in terms of a period of satiety.

Withdrawal from SOL began for Anu about 1974, and she abandoned the last study-circles three years later. However, leaving the town and moving to the country did not suffice to make the break. Anu had earlier joined the Communist Party, and this affiliation followed her faithfully. Sometimes she even went to the meetings of her party cells without finding much sense either in participating or trying to debate with her aging comrades. For these reasons, and due to the feelings of guilt or of inadequacy for not having done anything to change the state of affairs, she paid her last membership fees to the party around the mid-1980s. Was she withdrawing from the movement during these ten years?

In fact, the pattern of gradual fading out of the movement was not at all exceptional. Quite the contrary – if anything was a rare case among the stories I collected, it was an abrupt break. At the very least this seems to indicate an amazingly deep and complex involvement in the movement, capable of resisting satiety and growing political indifference. Withdrawal begins to resemble less and less a distinct personal conversion and more and more a story of flight: 'when I moved away I hoped that . . . no one would find me again [laughter]'. This reading seems to imply slow paradigm shifts, but not much in the way of conversion.

COHERENCE REGAINED

The results will be somewhat different if we try to read the rhetoric of coherence, or the key metaphors, organising the different parts of the story. In her first sentence, while answering my question about her present relationship to politics, Anu put it succinctly: 'I take myself to be nowadays a rather unpolitical person.' The last sentence of the interview returns to the theme: 'As the person who I am now and what I think . . . I don't act that way and of course I wouldn't go along with such things any more and I don't long for it.'

Both sentences attend to the same issue: *Who am I? What kind of a person am I?* Anu continues this reflection by asking what kind of person she was *supposed* to be in the organisation. The theme of the story is, therefore, her personal identity versus the identity imposed by the organisation. Rhetorically she differentiates the concept of 'the self' from 'the imposed self'. During the whole story she marks out the distance between herself as protagonist and her real self. Only through recognising this as the rhetoric of continuity and coherence is the reader enabled to see the story as drama, to understand her criticism of SOL, and to appreciate the sharp turns in her life course that are presented in the story.

The deepest disappointments that Anu experienced during her years of activism concerned her feelings of inability to be herself. She had expected people to understand her or to accept her as she was, but in vain. Acceptance was gained by consenting and supporting pre-existing policies, not by imagining oneself as a provider of new standpoints. However, the problem was not just her discomfort over the way that certain disturbing themes were excluded. Even more problematic was the idealised type of personality, or better, the identity imposed by the organisation. 'And another thing I personally suffered from . . . was . . . a sort of, let's say, that type or image of such a fighting young person, his personality, that ideal. It did violence to so many people, and surely also to me.'

Anu Rantanen's self-conception thus came into conflict with the identity promoted by the organisation. The problem was – as Anu puts it – that any local issue under consideration had to be elevated into the context of national or world politics. This concept of politics, so famous from Lenin's *What Is to Be Done?*, led her to use someone else's language in everyday discussions. The contradiction, therefore, did not lie just between the member and the organisation but rather the struggle for selfhood became an internal problem as well:

> somehow you had to put on borrowed clothes . . . . I tried to do it for so many years, let's say some three or four years at least, perhaps, [that] I rather actively tried to be different from what I am. And it seems to me that it was . . . I mean, I suffered from it because I felt that it is alien to me.

Borrowed clothes and the language of someone else are extremely strong metaphors of self-alienation. Anu felt herself unfit for the identity and tasks of a Leninist agitator, propagandist and organiser, and this turned out to be disastrous for her self-confidence within the movement. Of course, her story can also be read the other way round: the organisation may well have been able to strengthen the self-assurance of those activists fitting in better with this ideal type. For Anu Rantanen the situation was a dead end. As far as she was herself, she was not accepted, but trying to become the ideal type made her feel bad. No solution was satisfying. The narrator compresses the picture of those days in a laconic remark by noting that, nevertheless, she survived.

Despite the only very slow changes in her outward political orientation, Anu's story of the years 1974–76 seems to reveal a much sharper change. After discussing her withdrawal from SOL for a long time, I put a further question to her about periods in her life that she would possibly call 'crises'. She accepted the term and after a little while made it more specific:

> Let's say in the year '76, [I realise that] I've made such wrong solutions and choices, I've not had the courage to be what I am, and I've not acted the way I would have wanted to do and should've done, instead I've tried something else and I've been banging my head against a brick wall . . . . One had a feeling, though in several ways, that . . . I'm sure not to try anything which . . . doesn't seem to be something that I really stand for . . . or know what it is all about.

In the course of those few years, Anu experienced her 'trials in marriage' and the birth of her daughter. I take it that her extremely compressed account of her marriage covers a truly problematic, even if not entirely frustrating, experience, not ready to be narrated. Besides Lenin, Anu's daughter was the only person mentioned by name during the whole interview. Time after time, that is, in her marriage, studies and political activity, her orientation had turned out to be deeply wrong. In this story of the self, the turning point is clear and takes place in 1976.

The decisive turn in Anu Rantanen's life did not concern her party affiliations directly or questions of ideology but rather her relationship to her self and her identity. In the organisations she found more and more experiences that she no longer actually wanted to have. What she wanted, as she ironically put it, was to disappear, to become forgotten. What she wanted was a total paradigm shift. What she met instead was the iron mask of all orthodox identities: they do not allow any value or dignity to deviating identities, which are condemned either as perversity, heretics or betrayal (Connolly 1991).

Anu could not fight for her true self and her identity in her party cell. The reason for this was simple enough: she was not a 'young person looking for a fight'. During the ten-year moratorium she actually tried to be faithful to her self-image, to the image of a self-effacing woman. Silence and avoidance of drama fitted well with the 'myth of self' she had constructed during the crisis of 1976 (cf. Griffin 1990: 162).

After locating the turning point in Anu's life and the concomitant myth she constructed about herself, my analysis can proceed both forwards and backwards from this point (Denzin 1989: 67–8). Anu had mentioned how certain themes that she had promoted had been dropped from the official agenda. I asked her to give examples, one of which was the gender issue. Shortly afterwards, I asked again about the way that she had taken an interest in this issue. Typically, Anu began with a relational comment by locating herself among other women ('I also had reasons here in terms of my own personal history, as most of the women have'), and then she returns to her childhood:

> Practically, my mother was in a way a single parent, and I was the only girl in the family. We had four or five children, four sons, and then I was the only daughter, and my experience was . . . that I had to take such an emotional responsibility in that family . . . and I felt it was due to my sex . . . I felt it was wrong . . . and I struggled strongly against being a girl until I was probably about twelve years old . . . . I refused to put any skirts on or to play with girls and so on.

My point here is not to explain Anu's later experiences in SOL by these early feelings of problematic identity. Rather it is Anu herself who offers above a very strong causal argument. She presents herself now as a conscious fighter for her own identity who has always been sensitive to the problem of 'borrowed clothes'. The struggle for identity was of great importance in her childhood, and the case was exactly the same during her crises within SOL.

What Anu has achieved with her unifying rhetoric of the self and her struggle for identity is to provide her life story with a substantial amount of coherence and continuity. The discontinuities that she experienced during the 1970s, though dramatic and almost tragic, are finally only temporary (Linde 1993). This concern with identity even helped her to join SOL: 'when I took part in my first gatherings and so on, I perhaps met women of that sort so it was one reason I originally came along'. There was a promise of a new female identity in the movement, yet Anu was disappointed, and in the movement the contribution made by women was neglected. Her conclusion was that whether at home, at work or in the movement, women will have the same responsibilities. Arrangements in 'our organisation' were made in the same way as in the whole society. In Anu Rantanen's story women were either invisible, unsuitable characters or nurses for men:

> one had a bad feeling somehow from seeing so many women hanging around there, and who in a way gave their support but . . . they were not listened to and their views didn't get much weight . . . . It was very important to us . . . that those who act like that, who then, in a way, are such reliable comrades, who can be elected to different organs . . . and have the qualities required, they were always of the sort that excluded these women.

Again, in referring to a negative feeling, Anu uses the third person as a distancing and sheltering device. However, Anu did not regard just herself as an alien; the identity promoted by the organisation was seldom found to fit any woman. Anu supported a different politics of identity. She insisted that it is not always reasonable simply to fit easily into old political settings and structures; it might be more profitable to deviate from the given identity patterns. Instead of being unpolitical, Anu promoted a politicalisation of 'political identities'.

In contrast to the supposed chaos of Anu's narrative, I have presented two central methods of framing a life story: *explanation* as a way of answering problematic questions, and the *rhetoric of self and struggle for identity*. Linde (1993: 163–91) discusses a further method of finding coherence: 'coherence systems'. These systems are a popularised version of professional discourses which experts are using, located between common sense and expert systems. A 'coherence system is a system that claims to provide a means for understanding, evaluating, and constructing accounts of experience' (Linde 1993: 164). The story of Anu Rantanen fits in very well with Linde's first and almost only example, 'popular Freudian psychology'. Linde's first two criteria can be seen in this story:

1 splitting the self into components that are in disagreement;
2 the notion that real causes are to be found in childhood and childhood experiences;
3 the notion of levels of personality, some of which are deeper than others (Linde 1993: 167).

However, what makes all of this *a system*? It is pertinent to Linde's definition that popular Freudian psychology seems to be almost the only practicable example of her 'systems of coherence'. Feminism is the second-best example. However, with Linde's criteria, even the feminist coherence system fits the story of Anu quite well. This extremely narrow range of available coherence systems limits the usefulness of Linde's approach. My focus on individual rhetorics of coherence allows for a wider range of alternatives. Speakers like Anu may very well employ rhetoric based on popularised versions of known expert systems, but others may apply idiosyncratic versions of rhetoric as well. Linde sees narrators as embedded in quasi-expert systems; I see them as exploiters of various rhetorical resources.

Now it is time for a critical question. Does the search for coherence imply an ideological bias in favour of coherence? Does coherence reside in the story, or is it only a construction derived from the reader's need to find this coherence?

I argued above that the final coherence of a story is always constructed in its reception. Realist readers might have focused instead on the radical turns in Anu Rantanen's life, and then emphasised the lack of coherence. However, Linde's approach to coherence, or the rhetoric I identify, does not, by any means, exclude incoherences of life or life story. It is precisely the rhetoric of the self which Anu uses that enables the reader to distinguish the genuine turns of her life story. The coherence of the story does not presuppose any straightforward unity of the life. In contrast, radical turns in life, and problematic experiences in particular, call for the most sophisticated methods of creating coherence.

FROM 'THICKNESS' OF DESCRIPTION TO 'THICKNESS' OF EXPECTATIONS

During the interview, Anu gives several clues to her interpreter. She remarks repeatedly that she has not thought over her past. It is often more difficult to recollect actual events or topics of conversations, she points out, than what she felt at the time. The radical divide between present narrator and past protagonist is the source of all narrative reflection in life stories. Anu Rantanen the narrator sees the protagonist Anu Rantanen often as an enigma who perhaps acted and felt in the narrated way. Remembering and forgetting, of course, are not a purely cognitive problem. Anu views remembering as something that she should perhaps undertake sometime:

> sometimes I have such phases and situations, I think, one should somehow think over . . . phases of her life and ponder why one has made such and such choices in this and that phase of her life but so far I haven't done it, anyway. Either it has seemed too difficult or it has not seemed the right time yet . . . . Or, I don't know . . . . Perhaps it's something one cannot do at least by oneself.

The end of the section, with its new provisions, is left enigmatic. Perhaps the past 'I' and past events are unrecoverable? Or, on the other hand, does it mean that one is not always capable of remembering the past as it was? The deeply problematic nature of the past does not easily disappear. These comments leave the story and its interpretation in a permanent state of flux.

The fact that Anu's remembering is only half-finished partly accounts for the observed 'thinness' of the interview. Anu remembers that she has not discussed the whole theme for years. The 'thinness' of the story is part of the situation to be interpreted, not a sign of flatness in the material. If the 'thickness' of the descriptions is regarded as the central indicator of the credibility of the material, there will then be serious problems when confronted with an equally 'thick' charged silence.

'Thickness' as defined above by Denzin can be redefined as 'thickness of description', which does not quite fit the theoretical depth that Clifford Geertz (1973) originally assigned to the term. More recently linguistic research into narrative has revealed a great deal about how the 'point of a story' is actually delivered. William Labov (1972) distinguished both *orientational* descriptions and *evaluative* expressions from the basic narrative. His follower Deborah Tannen (1979) coined the term 'evidence of expectations' while referring to evaluative expressions, such as repetition, negatives, hedges, contrasting conjunctions, evaluative verbs ('sulking') and so on, in the same way. For example, a negative sentence informs us not only about what happened but also – and this is important – *what was expected* to happen. In a political world, the expectations of the various actors are far more important than, say, the details of the furniture in a meeting room. Following Labov and Tannen, I suggest that it is reasonable to talk about 'thickness of expectation' as an alternative to 'thickness of description'. The story of Anu Rantanen is extremely 'thick' in terms of both evaluations and expectations, indeed it is a story of failed and changed expectations.

SELF AND CONVENTION

Of course, the rhetoric of the self is a very conventional way of expressing one's own development, at least since the birth of psychoanalysis. Some of the same expressions were employed in the rhetoric of romanticism: 'It was only after years of anxiety, when I finally pulled myself together and began to be myself again' (Rousseau 1979: 57).

In the context of SOL, however, this rhetoric of the self marked a radical move leading to conflict with Marxist–Leninist discourse. The programmatic speech of SOL was dominated by a strong 'we' rhetoric and the need to be incorporated in greater and greater totalities. Anu's move, even though it appeared to take place as far away from politics as possible, was still concerned with the viability of staying in the movement. The new vocabulary and the independent politics of identity made activism in SOL extremely difficult.

The nature of the past can be defined by narrative style. Festive moments in the past, and the spirit of revolution, might raise feelings of nostalgia and longing for the good old days in the midst of the dull present. It is hard to find any trace of nostalgia in Anu Rantanen's story, which is totally free of the euphoric vocabulary and official icons of the movement: 'the year 1968' as well as 'the 1960s' and 'the struggle for [university] administration reform' do not appear in her speech.

A *romance* would be an alternative which offers the story of the protagonist as a continuous and heroic struggle with bigger and bigger social challenges, proceeding through a series of rites to do with status upheaval (Murray 1989). In a *comedy*, by contrast, the rites are about status reversal. As Kenneth Burke put it in his *Attitudes Toward History* (1984: 41): 'When you add that people are necessarily mistaken, that all people are exposed to situations in which they must act as fools, that every insight contains its own special kind of blindness, you complete the comic circle.' It is easy to see that the hero of Anu Rantanen does not act in a romance, but that a black comedy is much closer to her style.

In the worst case, the movement would have been a tragedy 'which destroyed my life'. The consciousness of a tragedy, and in particular tragedy as the fate of some other activists, is present but always redefined by irony ('Nevertheless, one survived it'). Anu Rantanen's personal style is paradoxical. She compresses the narrating part of her speech to a minimum, distances herself in expression by using analytical explanation, and then brings closeness back into play by presenting a history of her own feelings and the self.

Finally in conclusion, can one speak of her case as a *conversion narrative*? The smoothness of all the changes in her narrative tells against this interpretation. Nevertheless, I conclude that it is the very category of 'conversion narrative' that needs to be reformulated in accordance with the narrative concepts explored in this chapter. The radical turn in the story of the protagonist and the respective shift of paradigm do not wholly define the very character of the narrative as 'conversion'. There is once again the question of *attitude* and *voice*: *A conversion story presents a radically changed protagonist whose sins and weaknesses are displayed by the punishing narrator*. The core of this narrative form is the almost sadistic relationship between the narrator and protagonist, and the constant performance of repentance. This definition fits Colson's case very well, and also fits the story of St Augustine, but it does not fit the ironic sensibility of the narrator Anu Rantanen. None the less, her narration invokes a rhetoric of thorough political and personal change.

In this chapter, I have presented my sixth reading (within the last four years) of the very same interview. Every reading has introduced a more and more political Anu Rantanen. According to my experience as a revisionist of my own interpretations, the pure intuition of the reader does not have much to do with these transformations. (One aspect I have neglected in this chapter is the relational character of my changed interpretations, arising from patient commentary on my texts from a number of other readers.) Theoretical and methodological presuppositions ('thickness', conversion) have set frames which turned out to be laborious to break down. What I now call my deeper acquaintance with the story of Anu Rantanen has resulted from some new methodological considerations (e.g. expectational 'thickness', the role of explanation as a discursive unit). Nevertheless, my aim is neither to achieve a final analysis of this story nor a complete methodology for the study of life stories.

There are always new areas to be covered by agile political scientists. Even though flexibility is a great virtue, my experience of re-reading one and the same story in the course of these four years has offered me a useful methodological school for transforming my own concepts. The unyielding resistance of the story of Anu Rantanen made all of this possible. She did not narrate just to entertain her listener. As her comments about the male leaders of the movement or about 'the attempt of marriage' tell us very directly, she had particular reservations concerning a male interviewer who came from the same movement. Some other day, the story might have been different, as Anu told me afterwards. But this time, the pains of remembering and telling were articulated in an unforgettable way.

I want Anu to have the last word, and so I quote her words after the interview. Am I entitled to read them as a task given to me?

> Why do they always talk about the unity of the movement? At least on the cell level there were disagreements and debates on goals and the means by which to achieve them. People had in their minds an image of what it was all about in the movement. But everyone had a different image, and the reality never corresponded to this image exactly, so that you always had to revise your image.

4 Sex and discourse
The politics of the *Hite Reports*

Véronique Mottier

INTRODUCTION

The feminist slogan 'the personal is political' expresses the idea that many of women's 'personal' life experiences are in fact rooted in the subordinated position occupied by women as a group within the gendered power structure. It is within the context of this politicisation that sexual experiences have been discussed and problematised. While sexuality remained only a secondary issue during the first feminist wave (Weeks 1989), it became one of the central issues of the second wave. It is present in an important part of feminist claims during the last twenty-five years, including the right to sexual pleasure, the right to say 'no' (to refuse sexual advances), lesbianism as a political choice, and the issues of contraception, abortion, rape, pornography, incest and sexual harassment. Thus, feminist discourse endeavoured to introduce the 'politics of sex' into the political arena – and often succeeded.

Of course, the feminist problematisation of sexuality, as an attempt to transform power relations between the sexes, cannot be seen as a unified whole. Since Kate Millett's *Sexual Politics* (1970), multiple and diverging voices have participated in the debate. In this chapter, I propose to concentrate on one of the voices that has contributed to the feminist politicisation of sexuality, namely that of Shere Hite. While the *Hite Reports* (1976, 1981, 1987, 1994) treat most of the issues that have been raised by feminists over the past two decades, and in turn have contributed to the diversification and intensification of the debate, I do not mean to claim that they represent the whole of feminist thought on sexuality. Rather, I will analyse them as one voice among others.

The *Hite Reports* are embedded in a double discursive context. On the one hand, they are linked to the feminist politicisation of sexuality. While authors like Millett (1970) and Firestone (1972) have pointed to male control of women's sexuality, other feminists have stressed the violent forms that this control can take (Brownmiller 1975). Pornography has been rejected by many – though not all – feminists as a manifestation of this violence (see, e.g., Dworkin 1981, 1988; Griffin 1981). Women's sexual relationship to their own bodies has been explored from a lesbian perspective by writers such as Daly (1984) and Rich (1983). Hite's perspective on sexuality – as a reflection of the power relations between men and women – as well as her focus on women's relation to their own bodies, can be located within this field of feminist writings on sexuality.

On the other hand, the *Hite Reports* are also embedded in a scientific tradition of research on sexuality and are related to the progressive redefinition of sexuality, particularly as inaugurated by Kinsey (Kinsey *et al.* 1949, 1953). For a long time, sex research had considered female sexuality as a simple response to male instinct (Weeks 1989). By investigating female sexuality as an autonomous research object, Kinsey opened up new ways of studying and interpreting both male and female sexuality. This path was further pursued by sexologists like Fisher, Kaplan, Sherfey and Hite herself, as well as by Friday's (1973, 1975, 1980) studies of male and female sexual fantasies.

More broadly, Hite's work can be seen as a contribution to the history of the female body and its constitution as a site of sexual pleasure. Like Koedt (1973), she especially targets the 'myth of the vaginal orgasm', which in her view reflects men's dominance over women by imposing male norms of sexual pleasure. The 'myth of the vaginal orgasm' can be retraced to Freud. As Laqueur (1989) demonstrates, prior to Freud's distinction between clitoral and vaginal orgasm, Western medical as well as pornographic literature did not stress any kind of female orgasm other than the clitoral sort.

By claiming that sexual relations between men and women reflect the structure of power relations between the 'weaker' and the 'stronger' sex, the *Hite Reports* construct sexuality as a political issue. Their aim is to mobilise against dominant definitions of sexuality and of women's bodies, which are considered oppressive to women. Through questioning of the dominant discourse on sex, Hite means to challenge existing gender relations, proposing a different politics of sex. The main questions that I want to focus on are the following. How does this struggle define itself? What is its internal logic? What are the discursive strategies that are adopted in the *Hite Reports* in their challenge to dominant discourse on sexuality? With these questions as a starting point, it should be pointed out that the *Hite Reports* present themselves as a discourse of resistance, struggling against and breaking away from dominant – interpreted as male – sexual norms.

This does not mean that this struggle should indeed be considered in terms of a binary logic of domination and resistance, but rather as taking place within a more complex network of shifting power relations. As has been argued before (see De Lauretis 1987; Felski 1989), the simplifying conceptualisation of women as passive victims of patriarchal structures of domination, where men 'have the power' and women do not, should be abandoned in favour of a more complex and differentiated framework of analysis. While sharing these concerns, my aim is to bring to light the discursive logic that the *Hite Reports* follow, rather than to assess the framework that they use in terms of its adequacy for analysing the relations between gender and power. In particular, I want to ask what relationship to truth is involved in this self-avowed discourse of resistance.

Political discourses that aim for resistance and contestation can be grounded in different ways. Discursive strategies can, for instance, be grounded in a claim to science, like Marxism, or through a claim about subjectivity, like much of feminist thought. With regard to this central question of the relationship between discourse, foundations and truth, the *Hite Reports* are very interesting phenomena. Indeed, the relationship to truth is crucial for understanding the type of discursive strategies developed by the *Reports*. As to the justificatory dimension of this discourse, it will be shown that resistance is grounded on an interplay between science and subjectivity. While Hite bases her claims on the authority of science, her 'scientific' results – in her view – are further legitimised by their grounding in subjective experience.

The perspective that I bring to the *Hite Reports* is inspired by Foucault's work in two ways. First, I want to show how the *Reports* fit into the politics of sex broadly conceived. In this chapter, I propose a Foucauldian reading of the *Hite Reports*, considered as a counter-discourse within the network of power relations between the sexes. Second, I also want to show how the *Hite Reports* implicitly mimic aspects of a Foucauldian approach themselves. This does not mean that I consider the *Reports* on the whole to be a Foucauldian type of discourse – nor do I think that they necessarily should be. With respect to the conceptualisation of power relations, but also from the point of view of the methods that Hite uses in her investigations of sexuality – an important point that I will return to later – Hite's strategies are quite un-Foucauldian. However, other aspects of Hite's discourse are surprisingly similar to some of Foucault's ideas, as will be demonstrated. It is possible that Hite was familiar with Foucault's work, or vice versa. Nevertheless, in the absence of any acknowledgement of such an influence, it can just as plausibly be suggested that Hite and Foucault arrived independently at similar arguments. Hite herself notes with respect to similarities between her work and Foucault's: 'Scholars citing Foucault as the originator of this thesis should be careful to note accurately the earlier statement of this theory in *The Hite Report*' (Hite 1987: 236). While Hite refers here to the 1978 English translation of Foucault's *History of Sexuality*, vol. 1, it should be noted that this book was first published in French in 1976, the same year as *The Hite Report on Female Sexuality*.

POWER, KNOWLEDGE, ETHICS

In the *History of Sexuality*, vol. 1, Foucault develops an interpretative approach to sexuality combining a 'genealogical' method with an 'analytics of power', thus neglecting (though temporarily) the 'archaeological' dimension of his previous work. Genealogy is characterised in the first instance by the fact that it consists of a critical interpretation (Foucault 1972b, 1986a), a questioning of 'that which we assume to have always been the case' (Poster 1986: 208; see also Visker 1990). In volume 1, Foucault challenges what he calls the 'repressive hypothesis', the customary interpretation of the history of sexuality as one of an increasing repression of sex since the seventeenth century, halted only recently. According to Foucault, discourses on sex have, on the contrary, been subjected to institutional mechanisms that increasingly incite discursive production. The main examples of this are the Church (through confession, for instance), the state (which 'discovers' population as a source of wealth and thus as a target for intervention, notably with regard to the regulation of procreation for economic and political reasons), as well as pedagogy, medicine, psychiatry, etc. Sex becomes an object of knowledge, a 'truth issue'. The avowal of the 'truth' about sex is provoked through confession in all its various modes and sites, which Foucault considers the essential procedure for the production of truth in the West.

The second characteristic of genealogical method in volume 1 of the *History of Sexuality* concerns the analytic grid which is being applied. This grid maps out the relations between discourse, knowledge and power, taking into account not only the 'negative', repressive side of power, but also its 'positive' – in the sense of 'productive' – side. This latter works through confessionary techniques of power, 'sites of power/knowledge' like psychiatry or pedagogy, which provoke the production of discourses charged with pretensions to truthfulness. This is because, as happens during confession, the interrogated subject must speak the truth. The truth thus lies in sex, which arises from 'the will to know' which characterises Western societies, so Foucault argues (see Foucault 1978, 1994b: 256 ff.).

The third characteristic of genealogy concerns the notion of origin: the aim is to analyse the birth of experiences such as sexuality, but this is accompanied by a Nietzschean refusal to find an 'essence', an original sexuality which one should uncover (Foucault 1972b, 1978; Davidson 1986). It is the making of sexuality through the articulation of discourse, power and knowledge that creates a certain historical experience of sexuality. If genealogy challenges customary interpretations, it does so without presenting a 'point zero' in the past as an alternative (Poster 1986). Nietzsche's influence on Foucault in this regard has been important (see Deleuze 1986; Dreyfus and Rabinow 1982; Eribon 1994; Foucault 1986a, 1994a; Thiele 1990; Visker 1990). However, I agree with Thiele (1990: 923) that there has been a selective adaptation, rather than an uncritical adoption of Nietzsche's ideas in Foucault's work.

Foucault combines his genealogical approach with an 'analytics' of power. He conceptualises power as an open network of relations, containing no central point, but rather multiple foci of power which give rise to corresponding points of resistance. According to what he calls his 'strategic model of power', power relations do not represent a permanent structure, but rather a given moment of a continuing process. In Foucault's perspective, the distribution of power and the appropriation of knowledge is unstable. Relations of power/knowledge are constantly shifting, and form what Foucault (1978) calls 'matrices of transformation' along which power and knowledge are continuously redistributed, rather than static structures.

The subsequent volumes of Foucault's history of sexuality move away from the analytical axes of knowledge and power (to the chagrin of some, cf. Poster 1986), and instead concentrate on a third axis, namely ethics. The ethical axis corresponds to the study of the

historical ways in which individuals recognise themselves as subjects, and as sexual subjects in the case of the history of sexuality
(Foucault 1985, 1986b).

In order to understand the discursive strategies developed by the
Hite Reports for transforming power/knowledge relations, I take
into account his three analytical axes: power, knowledge and ethics.
I consider the *Hite Reports* as a focus of power, or rather of
counter-power, within the network of power/knowledge relations
which, as we have seen, do not correspond to a permanent structure
but rather a process of distribution. These relations form matrices
of transformation along which power/knowledge positions are
refigured. Feminist discourse acts upon the matrix of power/knowl-
edge relations concerning sexuality by problematising them as they
are transformed. This is understood in the sense defined by
Foucault (Kritzman 1988: 257) as 'the totality of discursive or non-
discursive practices that introduces something into the play of true
and false and constitutes it as an object for thought (whether in the
form of moral reflection, scientific knowledge, political analysis,
etc.)'. The main goal of my analysis is to understand through which
'discursive strategies' – Foucault develops this concept in *The
Archaeology of Knowledge* (1972a) – Hite contributes to the feminist
problematisation of sexuality. (I present a more thorough discussion
of Foucault's conceptualisation of power, and its use for analysing
feminist discourse on sexuality, in another article, which treats different aspects of the *Hite Reports* – see Mottier 1994.)

An archaeological dimension will allow me to grasp the 'points
of problematisation', by asking questions such as: through which
issues is sexuality problematised in the *Hite Reports*, and what
forms does this problematisation take? The archaeological dimension will then be complemented by a genealogical one, focusing on
the positive (in the Foucauldian sense of productive) aspects of the
Hite Reports. What construction of sexuality do the latter mean to
produce through the problematisation of certain aspects of sex?
Which are the sexual practices of the self included within this feminist definition of sexuality?

THE *HITE REPORTS*

Points of problematisation

My analysis is based on *The Hite Report on Female Sexuality*
(1976), *The Hite Report on Male Sexuality* (1981), *Women and Love:*

The Hite Report on Love, Passion and Emotional Violence (1987) and *The Hite Report on the Family: Growing Up Under Patriarchy* (1994). In the *Hite Reports*, the problematisation of sexuality concentrates on the following issues: one's relationship with one's own body, with the other sex, with one's own sex, and with truth. These points of problematisation closely resonate with those observed by Foucault (1985, 1988) in ancient Greek and Roman discourses. Hence, a similar discursive structure characterises the problematisation of sex within very different historical contexts. This commonality is nevertheless limited, because the forms taken by the problematisation and, in particular, the discursive construction of sex resulting from it, are quite different. The relationship with one's body, with the other sex, with the same sex and with truth are the main problems which Hite's questionnaires address in investigating sexual behaviour. The *Hite Reports* also construct a counter-interpretation of what sexuality should consist in with respect to this set of issues. At the same time, it is the 'scientific' investigation of these points of power/knowledge that leads to their ethical problematisation.

Forms of problematisation: the relationship with one's own body

The problematisation of the relationship with one's own body is present in various forms in the *Hite Reports*. It mainly takes the form of an investigation of the capacity to produce pleasure in one's own body (the issue of masturbation); of bodily pleasures in various degrees of intensity; of mastering of one's own body (the issue of contraception, but also of the right to pleasure); of the relationship between body and emotions, as well as of the changing relationship with one's own body (in particular under the influence of ageing). However, while these issues can be found in the investigation in the *Reports* of male as well as female sexuality, the extent of problematisation may vary.

This is particularly clear with regard to the issue of pleasure given to one's own body. Whereas it occupies an entire chapter of the *Report* on female sexuality, its importance as a research object becomes very secondary in the *Report* on men. Indeed, within the argument in the *Report* on female sexuality, this issue plays a strategic role. One of the conclusions of Hite's 'scientific' investigation of sexuality is that most women are capable of producing pleasure in their own bodies by stimulating themselves. 'Of the 82 percent of women who say they masturbated', Hite contends, '95 percent could orgasm easily and regularly, whenever they wanted' (Hite 1976: 59). This research result is then used as an argument for challenging the 'dominant' interpretation of sex, which – after defining sexuality mainly through intercourse – had, according to Hite, arrived at the conclusion that many women are 'frigid'. On the contrary, Hite argues that as most women seem to be quite capable of experiencing sexual pleasure, the problem is not so much what Masters and Johnson (1970) term female 'coital orgasmic inadequacy', but rather the way in which sexual norms are defined.

> The fact that women can orgasm easily and pleasurably whenever they want (many women several times in a row) shows beyond a doubt that women know how to enjoy their bodies; no one needs to tell them how. It is not female sexuality that has a problem ('dysfunction') but society that has a problem in its definition of sex and the subordinate role which that definition assigns to women.
>
> (Hite 1976: 60)

> Sex as we know it is a 'male-defined activity', and women – in not showing enthusiasm for many aspects of it – are displaying resistance to participation in an institution which they have not had an equal part in creating.
>
> (Hite 1981: 732)

There seems to be a certain ambiguity in Hite's argument on this point. On the one hand, whereas research on sexual relations between men and women has usually led to the problematisation of women's bodies, the *Hite Reports* investigate women's bodies in order to challenge the dominant norms concerning sex between men and women. The *Hite Reports* thus illustrate how points of power/knowledge such as women's bodies can be articulated differently at different foci of power/knowledge. Within different discursive contexts, women's bodies can be subjected to oppressive normalising practices and discourses, but they can also be articulated as points of resistance and a basis for counter-claims. On the other hand, while Hite challenges the habitual problematisation of women's bodies, she also prolongs it. The point I want to make is that Hite substitutes one interplay between pleasure, power and knowledge for another, while spelling out a contrasting ethical task for both men and women that continues to focus sexual and discursive attention on women's bodies:

If you can't orgasm, you could also read books on sex therapy, feminist literature, and try to talk to friends about how they have orgasms. You could also try a local women's self-help group, perhaps a sex-therapist, or a lover who was sensitive enough to help. *Don't give up*. Many women *have* learned to orgasm after years of not knowing how, and it is never too late to discover what works for *you*.

(Hite 1976: 222)

To have an orgasm during intercourse, there are two ways a woman can increase her chances, always remembering that she is adapting her body to less than adequate stimulation. First and most important, she must consciously try to apply her masturbation techniques to intercourse, or experiment to find out what else may work for her to get clitoral stimulation; or, she can work out a sexual relationship with a particular man who can meet her individual needs.

(Hite 1976: 301)

Forms of problematisation: the relationship with the other sex

Hite conceptualises her own discourse as a discourse of resistance against dominant, male definitions of sexuality, following a binary opposition between oppressed (women) and oppressors (men). She argues: 'It is very clear by now that the pattern of sexual relations predominant in our culture exploits and oppresses women. . . . [It] has institutionalised out any expression of women's sexual feelings except for those that support male needs' (Hite 1976: 384).

From a theoretical perspective, Hite's use of binary representations of sexual power relations may appear unsatisfying. However, from the point of view of what Austin (1990) calls the 'performative value' of political discourse, the use of binary oppositions enhances discursive capacity for mobilisation. In other words, although Hite's discursive strategies may simplify reality, they serve her political aims. The binary opposition between men-the-oppressors and women-the-victims clearly indicates whose norms women must revolt against. 'It must have been clear throughout this book', Hite writes, 'how tired women are of the old mechanical pattern of sexual relations, which revolves around male erection, male penetration, and male orgasm' (Hite 1976: 529). She affirms:

This state of inner questioning, alienation, and frustration many women are experiencing – whether they stay in their relationship or leave – represents a long goodbye not only to the man in question but also to 'male' culture and to our allegiance to that culture's hold on us.

(Hite 1987: 625)

Hite's binary oppositions further mobilise in that they serve to homogenise both groups, downplaying internal differences. This polarising effect of Hite's discursive strategies is deepened by her use of strong metaphors regarding the oppression of women by male sexual norms. Women find themselves, Hite argues, in a state of 'sexual slavery' to men, providing them with sexual pleasure while ignoring their own needs. Hite is not the first to use this metaphor of 'slavery'. In Britain the expression was used, for example, during the militant suffragettes' campaign in 1912 against the double standard of sexual morality, which was attacked for treating women as the 'sexual slaves' of their husbands (see Jackson 1994). Hite says:

> The fact is that the role of women in sex, as in every other aspect of life, has been to serve the needs of others – men and children. And just as women did not recognise their oppression in a general sense until recently, just so sexual slavery has been an almost unconscious way of life for most women.

(Hite 1976: 419)

> Women are sexual slaves insofar as they are (justifiably) afraid to 'come out' with their own sexuality, and forced to satisfy others' needs and ignore their own.

(Hite 1976: 420)

This sexual slavery is seen as expressing the subordinated position of women within the gender power structure: 'A woman's place in sex mirrors her place in the rest of society' (Hite 1976: 11). And: 'Lack of sexual satisfaction is another sign of the oppression of women' (Hite 1976: 420). Moreover: 'This cultural denial of women's sexual needs reflects the larger social system in which women have been given second-class status for hundreds of years, and is part of the larger social problems between men and women' (Hite 1981: 616).

While the *Hite Reports* do not present all men as rapists, they do consider male sexual violence (almost exclusively discussed only as it is directed towards women) as symbolising masculine domination in general:

Sex/intercourse has traditionally been the basic symbol of male domination and ownership of women (whether or not an individual man may feel this at any given time). Rape and buying women through pornography are basic extensions of this ideology – not biologic 'urges' or part of a physical male 'sex drive'. It is what 'sex' means to men that makes them sometimes want to rape women, not a desire for orgasm.

(Hite 1981: 741)

Right now, forcible physical rape stands as an overwhelming metaphor for what has been the rape – physical, emotional and spiritual – of an entire gender by our culture.

(Hite 1981: 742)

In response to this oppression of women, Hite urges women to stop depending on men in order to achieve sexual satisfaction. The performative character of her argument is particularly present in this exhortation to women to regain control of their own bodies:

The taboo against touching yourself says essentially that you should not use your own body for your own pleasure, that your body is not your own to enjoy. But we have a right to our own bodies. Controlling your own stimulation symbolises owning your own body, and is a very important step toward freedom.

(Hite 1976: 386)

Is the 'answer' to the oppression and neglect of female sexuality and especially orgasm that men should learn to give (better) clitoral stimulation? Yes and no. Of course men should learn these things but, even more important, we should find the freedom to take control over whether or not we get this stimulation.

(Hite 1976: 354 ff.)

It is thus through the problematisation of relations with the other sex that women's relationship with their own bodies is questioned, albeit in a different way than in 'dominant' discourse: the problematisation of sexual relations with men challenges the fact that women make so little use of the possibilities for pleasure which their own bodies offer them. 'We know', Hite writes, 'how to have orgasms in masturbation. How strange it is, when you think of it, that we don't use this knowledge during so much of the sex we have with men' (Hite 1976: 385).

Forms of problematisation: the relationship with one's own sex

The problematisation of the relationship with one's own sex mainly takes the form of research on possible homosexual experiences. Hite argues that the social interdiction of physical relations between women acts negatively upon the possibilities for female solidarity:

> Vis-à-vis women's connection with one another, this ban on physical contact is oppressive and has the effect of separating women.
>
> (Hite 1976: 392; see also 1987: 586; 1994: 133 ff.)

The point here is that a prohibition on the exchange of physical contact (*of any kind*) between women is bound to increase the level of hostility and distance between them.

> (Hite 1976: 392)

The problematisation of sexual relations between women is thus part of a larger questioning of the relations between women in general. However, discourse on relations between women is also linked to a problematisation of sexual relations with men. As these latter relations are seen as mirroring male domination in general, sex between women is presented as permitting more equality between partners:

> Besides the increased affection and sensitivity and the increased frequency of orgasm, some women felt that sex with another woman could be better because of the more equal relationship possible. Sex with women can be a reaction against men and our second class status with them in this society.
>
> (Hite 1976: 414)

Lesbianism appears here as a possible way of refusing male domination. Hite thus takes on the idea of lesbianism as a political choice, which had been advanced by certain radical feminists. Nevertheless, Hite distances herself explicitly from the more extreme position that lesbianism *should* be chosen as the only really feminist option:

> It might be natural for any oppressed group to turn on those oppressing them and declare their own superiority. Actually, however, in a way relationships between women are superior. Still, it cannot be dictated to women that they 'should' cease being 'heterosexual' and become gay. Unfortunately, in some gay

circles there has been a holier-than-thou attitude directed by gay women at straight women.

(Hite 1987: 578)

Finally, Hite's discourse on relations between women also problematises women's relation with their own bodies. Indeed, the level of comfort that women feel with respect to other women's bodies is indicative, Hite contends, of women's feelings toward their own bodies:

> Any woman who feels actual horror or revulsion at the thought of kissing or embracing or having physical relations with another woman should re-examine her feelings and attitudes not only about other women, but also about *herself*. A positive attitude toward our bodies and toward touching ourselves and toward any physical contact that might naturally develop with another woman is essential to self-love and accepting our own bodies as good and beautiful.

(Hite 1976: 416)

In the *Report* on male sexuality, the question of homosexual experiences is linked to the problematisation of general relations between men, which are judged to be too distant and too unemotional. This type of relationship is interpreted as resulting from the same definition of 'masculinity' that characterises men's attitudes towards women. But, according to Hite, men suffer from this physical and emotional distance which separates them from other men, and especially from their fathers:

> A boy's relationship with his father . . . is crucial to the concept a boy learns of masculinity. Most men as a boy had a very distant relationship with their fathers. . . . Boys, knowing their fathers from such a distance, seeing them so reserved and unemotional, rarely passionate or 'overly' affectionate, frequently grew up believing that it is not 'masculine' to communicate openly or spontaneously about feelings. We have seen, and will see, that this affects men's relationship with other men and with women very profoundly.

(Hite 1981: 85)

The problematisation of relations between men is connected to a challenge to the male definition of sexuality, as well as to men's treatment of women. Hite writes:

Men could reach much higher peaks of arousal if they did not feel anxious about how they 'should' behave sexually, and if they did not focus so much on reaching orgasm. Men's denial of their great sensuality is significant because it is part of the overall denial by men of their feelings and emotions: a 'real' man, it is said, should learn to always be 'in control' of his emotions.

(Hite 1981: 477)

This issue contributes to the performative dimension of Hite's argument, which claims that changes in the definition of masculinity in general and of the male definition of sexuality in particular are both necessary. However, discourse on male homosexual experiences differs from that on lesbianism insofar as sexual relations between men are interestingly not interpreted as expressing a will to be independent from the other sex. This difference may be linked to Hite's binary representation of the relation between men and women. If women are represented as victims, oppressed by men, the latter would not seem to have any particular reason for wanting to avoid women. On the contrary, Hite suggests, men have everything to gain from being close to women: 'The happiest men in this study were those with the closest, most functioning relationships with women – that is, a minority of (in most cases married) men' (Hite 1981: 330).

Forms of problematisation: the relationship with truth

The relationship with truth constitutes the fourth point of the problematisation of sex in the *Hite Reports*. Underlying these texts as a whole, one finds the conviction that sexuality reflects the 'truth' of gender relations, the truth being relations of domination:

'Male' sexuality is central to the definition of masculinity – and masculinity is central to the world-view of the entire culture – in a sense, *is* the culture. Therefore, what we are looking at in this book is far more than male sexuality, it is a way of life, the world itself, a culture in microcosm.

(Hite 1981: xvii)

It is argued that sex expresses the truth of our being: who we are, who we want to be, our aspirations on a personal as well as on a societal level – which at the same time explains the importance given to this theme as object of research and of theorisation: 'To discuss sex is to discuss our most basic views of who we are, what we want life to be, and what kind of a society we believe in' (Hite 1981: xvii).

Taking this interpretation of sex as the locus of truth of our being-in-the-world, the goal of the *Reports* is to contribute to changing what has for a long time been the truth of gender relations. The final aim is to find new ways of living together, of living one's sexuality, alone or together. It is claimed that not only women, but also men would benefit from these changes. 'Some men', Hite contends, 'were beginning to see how their own welfare is tied up with women's fight to restructure their lives and relationships for the better' (Hite 1981: 330). She adds:

> Trying to live by the male code, being totally self-sufficient, emotionally and economically, always providing shelter and food (or sex and orgasms), never receiving or needing anything, never needing a woman's love more than she needs a man's – all this hurts and stunts men. Some men were beginning to see how their own welfare is tied up with women's fight to restructure their lives and relationships for the better. . . . 'Masculinity' can be just as much of a pressure on men as an enforced 'femininity' can be on women.
>
> (Hite 1981: 330; see also 1994: 340 ff.)

Knowledge forms an important stake with regard to this redefinition of gender relations. Within the *Hite Reports*, knowledge – and thus the relationship with truth – occupies a strategic position. At each discussion of one of the points of problematisation, Hite makes constant use of the knowledge furnished by her research. This knowledge serves in fact as counter-knowledge, challenging the dominant model of sexuality. It is through the problematisation of the relationship with truth that Hite attacks dominant truth claims, opposing 'true' sexuality, without domination, to the male-defined model of sexuality. The *Hite Reports* reject, for instance, what they consider to be the male interpretation of the so-called 'sexual revolution', which was said to represent more sexual freedom for everyone. In the *Reports* it is replaced by the claim that the sexual revolution has 'taken away women's right not to have sex' (Hite 1976: 457; see also 1987: 233 ff.). The possibility for women to refuse sex is interpreted not as expressing some kind of prudishness, or negative conditioning, but as a political act, explicitly compared to Gandhi's passive resistance (see Hite 1981: 734) and expressing 'a large-scale and healthy resistance to being dominated and to their bodies being owned' (Hite 1981: 734). Time after time, dominant truth claims are thus challenged by alternative ones, and knowledge – as expressed by the constative dimension of the texts – serves to legitimise claims on its performative level. Knowledge also appears as a resource from which readers – and especially women – might benefit. Indeed, the *Hite Reports* explicitly present themselves as a source of information on how women might make better use of their bodies, thus permitting them more independence from men on this point. 'I hope', Hite writes, 'that reading many of the things other women have said in this book will help' (Hite 1976: 222).

The *Reports* thus do not only mean to challenge current gender relations, but also to serve as a tool, as what Foucault (1985) calls an 'operator', enabling readers to question their relationship with themselves as well as with others through the problematisation of other individual's sexual experiences, that is, the ethical axis.

FROM SENSUALITY TO SEXUALITY

With respect to sexual knowledge, the *Hite Reports* thus frequently come close to resembling the discourse found in self-help literature, which explains how to become rich, how to do gardening, how to find a job, how to receive guests, how to stay slim and finally how to have a good sex life. Borrowing a concept developed by Giddens (1992: 30), one could say that the information provided by the *Reports* is intended to be a 'reflexive resource' that readers may draw upon in the reflexive making of their own sexuality reflexively. In this sense, it may be argued that the confessional techniques of knowledge production used by Hite ultimately aim to facilitate readers' reflexive incorporation of this same knowledge into their own everyday sexual practices, rather than to dominate the 'objects of study'. In other words, and using a rather un-Foucauldian vocabulary, one might say that the goal of the *Hite Reports* is emancipation rather than control. While the emancipatory aspects of self-help literature lead Giddens (1992: 28 ff.) to reject their confessional character altogether, I would argue instead that it is precisely because of this emancipatory dimension that such discourses may constitute foci of counter-power/knowledge. Within the network of shifting power–knowledge relations, confessional modes of knowledge production may indeed provide resources to foci of power as well as to counter-forces. At the same time, there remains a certain ambiguity with regard to the emancipatory dimension of the *Hite Reports*, in that they propose 'emancipation' from a particular set of relations with truth, from a particular set of codes of knowledge, and from a particular ethical regime into another.

Within the *Hite Reports*, the central issue of the self-help type of argument – addressed to women – seems to be 'how to reach orgasm', the main answer being 'do it yourself'. In case other women's experiences might not prove sufficient as a source of inspiration, explicit advice is often given, in passages such as 'Where should you stimulate yourself?' (Hite 1976: 215). In this way we can see how the practices of the 'new' sexuality are formulated. The aim is to modify dominant sexual practices, through problematising and challenging dominant discourse. Genealogical analysis allows us – taking the practices through which different sexual practices of the self should be constructed as a basis – to get a better understanding of what this alternative sexual paradigm would look like. Taking into account the positive (in the sense of 'creative') dimension of discourse, what do the *Hite Reports* create, or at least aim to create, by their problematisation of the dominant interpretations of sex? What alternative definition of sex do they propose?

As we have seen, Hite believes that dominant sexual norms exploit women, hence the claim that new, non-oppressive definitions of sexuality should be constructed. In fact, Hite does not aim at a simple redefinition, which would imply formulating sexuality differently but still taking existing norms as a starting point, thus remaining imprisoned within the conceptual framework of the dominant discourse on sex. Instead of this, she claims the necessity to go beyond the concept of sexuality itself, in order to be able to construct an entirely different sexual paradigm. The introduction of the term 'to un-define' in the final chapter of the *Report on Women*, entitled 'Toward a new female sexuality', illustrates the conceptual strategy adopted by the *Hite Reports*: 'What is really needed is a total redefinition, or that is, an un-definition, of sexuality' (Hite 1976: 537).

The *Hite Reports* thus construct the description of an experience that is no longer referred to as sexuality, but instead as 'sensuality', including not only those activities that are generally considered as being a part of sex, but also more general physical contacts. In addition, it is claimed that this experience cannot be conceptualised very well without taking into account emotions:

> While the point here is certainly not to say that sex must always be 'sweet', not passionate, the idea of sexuality as completely cut off from feeling – sex as something 'subhuman' that animals

(who have no feelings?) do and therefore not part of our humanity, part of a whole person – is a rather strange definition of sexuality, and probably not the most erotic one we could espouse.

(Hite 1987: 242)

However, sensuality is not presented as a new norm, but rather as indicating a set of possibilities: ' "Sex" could be un-defined to become something with infinite variety, not always including intercourse or even orgasm (for either person). It can become part of an individual vocabulary of many ways to relate physically' (Hite 1981: 477).

This sexual paradigm mainly selects the body and its pleasure as a starting point (and not, for instance, sexual identities or the type of partner). It can be noted that Hite's sexual paradigm, with its stress on pleasure, has a certain family resemblance to Giddens's concept of 'plastic sexuality' (see Giddens 1992). Hite says: 'Sex is intimate physical contact for pleasure, to share pleasure with another person (or just alone)' (Hite 1976: 528). In this respect, the *Hite Reports* strangely echo Foucault, who declares in the *History of Sexuality*, vol. 1: 'The rallying point for the counterattack against the deployment [*dispositif*] of sexuality ought not to be sex-desire, but bodies and pleasures' (Foucault 1978: 157).

CONCLUSION

I have looked at the way in which the *Hite Reports* construct sexuality as an object of study and, at the same time, as a target for feminist claims. Within the general framework of Foucault's discursive approach to sexuality, the *Hite Reports* can be considered as foci of discourse on sexuality, but at the same time as sources of incitement to the production of discourses. Their goal is to propose a new theorisation of sexuality by submitting the interrogated subjects to a 'will to know', inciting them to textual production. Therefore, these foci of discourse are at the same time also foci of power/knowledge, penetrating the body through power techniques, and provoking the formation of knowledge, that is, of truth claims: sex becomes an object of knowledge. The research tools that are being used – questionnaires in the case of the *Hite Reports* – aim to provoke the production of narratives of the sexual self. Through these confessionary techniques of power/knowledge, the 'truth' with regard to one's own personal sexual experiences is being produced.

However, the *Hite Reports* are also characterised by the fact that they conceptualise themselves as a critical discourse, breaking away from dominant interpretations of sex which are thought to reflect existing gender relations. While the goal of the *Hite Reports* is to establish 'better' knowledge of female sexuality, they also explicitly aim to use this subjugated knowledge in order to challenge dominant definitions of sexuality and to mobilise against them. The construction of sex as a research object is thus accompanied by its construction as an issue of struggle. This articulation of a constative dimension (taking the form of a 'scientific' argument) and of a performative dimension (mobilisation against dominant sexual norms) characterises the discursive strategies developed in the *Hite Reports*.

I want to argue that the Foucauldian concept of 'truth games' is very useful to further characterise the discursive strategies that are developed by Hite. In *The Use of Pleasure* (1985), Foucault insists on the importance of analysing 'the games of truth and error through which being is historically constituted as experience . . . . What are the games of truth by which man proposes to think his own nature when he perceives himself to be mad; when he conceives of himself as a living, speaking, labouring being; when he judges and punishes himself as a criminal?' (Foucault 1985: 7). Truth games are embedded in regimes of truth, which are historical, and which reflect power relations. From this perspective, Hite undertakes to question the current regime of truth, associated with the oppression of women, by causing existing sexual norms to enter the game of truth and falsity, thus constituting them as objects of scientific analysis, as well as of political struggle. By opposing alternative truth claims to existing ones, Hite undertakes to formulate new games of truth with which, to paraphrase Foucault, women and men propose to think their own nature when they perceive themselves as (sexual) beings.

The particular discursive strategy that Hite develops centres on the questioning of current truth claims. The alternative truth claims are argued with the help of the authority of her 'scientific' data, which are constantly referred to and serve a role of procedural legitimation. Notoriously Hite's study has been questioned as to whether it is indeed 'scientific', from the point of view of the positivist criteria that she herself invokes. However, this is not a question that I want to raise here, as my interest lies rather in analysing the strategic role played by these truth claims. While the interplay between political aims and statistical 'data' has been present ever since Quetelet's moral statistics (see Hacking 1991), it is particularly

central to Hite's truth games. This legitimation through science is
linked with a claim to subjective experience. Indeed, Hite's results
are presented as expressing experiences that had remained hidden
and silenced until then:

> Women have never been asked how they felt about sex.
> Researchers, looking for statistical 'norms', have asked all the
> wrong questions for all the wrong reasons – and all too often
> wound up telling women how they should feel rather than asking
> them how they do feel. . . . What these questionnaires have
> attempted to do is to ask women themselves how they feel, what
> they like, and what they think of sex.
>
> (Hite 1976: 11)

These experiences are not only used indirectly, in aggregated
form, but also directly through long quotations from the survey
answers. The truth games through which this particular discourse of
resistance undertakes to problematise male-defined sexuality are
thus discursively legitimised through a claim to subjugated
(counter-) knowledge:

> Like astronauts, we are moving ever farther away from the plan-
> et, now discerning the outlines of the system more clearly, seeing
> it for the first time as merely an ideological system, a set of
> beliefs with no right to define us – and so we no longer accept
> the definition of our 'place' by this ideology. We are self-naming
> and indeed beginning to name the rest of the culture, including
> 'male psychology' – and this in the midst of a dominant culture
> that still tells us we 'can't do this', that we are wrong.
>
> (Hite 1987: 644 ff.)

This is the resistance, the beginning of the change – when the
Other describes the dominant society, its ideology, for the first
time, names truly what was before taken to be 'human nature'
and inevitable.

> (Hite 1987: 678)

I have considered the *Hite Reports* as one of the agents of what
Foucault calls the putting-into-discourse (*mise en discours*) of sex,
and my main goal has been to analyse the characteristics presented
by this construction of sex through a type of argument which
claims to be a critical one. With regard to this aspect, we know
Foucault's famous critique towards self-claimed critical discourses
on sex. In his view, psychoanalysis and sexual liberation move-

ments, which are based on the idea that sex is subjected to oppression, could more plausibly be thought of as other ways of provoking confessions, provoking new discourses (Foucault 1994c: 527). These counter-discourses follow the same logic as the sources of power/knowledge which they claim to fight. From this perspective, it can be questioned to what extent the putting-into-discourse of sex by the *Hite Reports* forms a continuity with regard to the sources of power/knowledge that they claim to surpass. Are the discursive strategies developed by Hite comparable with those adopted by sexual liberation theorists?

By taking into account the three analytical axes of power, knowledge and ethics, I am led to argue that the discursive strategies followed by the *Hite Reports* do not strictly centre on a logic of oppression/liberation. For there is a certain ambiguity in Hite's discourse. On the one hand, in several passages of the *Hite Reports*, reference is made to the oppression of female sexuality, which does imply the idea of an oppressed sexual essence. On the other hand, elsewhere, there is an endeavour to go beyond the conceptual framework of 'sexuality'. This un-definition of sexuality in favour of sensuality starts out in the direction that Foucault (in Gordon 1980: 220; Foucault 1994b) indicates for a genuine critical discourse: that of a de-sexualisation, not based any more on sexual norms, but on bodily pleasures. In this respect, the alternative games of truth formulated by Hite and Foucault are not unproblematic. Hence the discursive strategies which the *Hite Reports* adopt in their challenge of the dominant politics of sex are quite Foucauldian. Against the construction of sexuality by dominant discourse, they aim to 'counter the grips of power with the claims of bodies, pleasures, and knowledges, in their multiplicity and their possibilities of resistance' (Foucault 1978: 157).

5 Aspects of Irish political culture
A hermeneutical perspective

Valerie Bresnihan

This chapter applies hermeneutic principles to selected aspects of Irish political culture. This is an exercise in what is called the 'hermeneutics of suspicion' and includes the deployment of narrative analysis and a structuralist method. My aim is to assess the symbolic associations attached to differing political thought systems in order to understand the dynamics of political change in contemporary Ireland.

I shall first provide a perspective on hermeneutics, that is, the hermeneutics of Gadamer and Ricoeur. Second, I shall identify three models of politics that may be relevant to Irish political culture. And finally I shall highlight certain aspects of psychoanalytic thinking and also employ a critical philosophy of history in order to understand the individual motivations at work within the three models of politics that I identified.

My starting point is the Irish presidential election campaign of 1990, described in the first section of this chapter. In effect I challenge the suggestion of O'Leary and Heskith that in Irish political culture 'liberal and traditional values exist side by side . . . [and] deserve much deeper examination' (O'Leary and Heskith 1988: 59). The results of my overall research project will show that the conclusions reached by the above authors are an elaborate oversimplification. The two value systems mentioned are inextricably intertwined and interdependent not only with each other but with other political value systems as well.

INTRODUCTION

The presidential election campaign

The presidential election campaign is the starting point of my research, and I begin by highlighting the most relevant points. On 7 September 1990, exactly one month from election day, the Irish presidential election campaign was still so dull and so unexciting that the *Irish Times* newspaper editorial stated, with more apparent hope than conviction, that 'the least the electorate deserves . . . is an exciting contest'. This is precisely what the electorate ultimately got. On 7 October 1990, Mary Robinson's completely unexpected electoral triumph represented what the media termed 'a turning point in Irish history'.

So what happened? The remit of this chapter prevents me from giving a lengthy description of this historic election campaign. Suffice it to say that the election of the seventh President of the Republic of Ireland witnessed the unexpected and emotive triumph of Mary Robinson, a declared feminist and a civil rights campaigner of some repute, as Ireland's first woman President. Her victory over Brian Lenihan, one of the most popular and genuinely paladin-type politicians of the largest political party, Fianna Fail, is perhaps best characterised by the following media descriptions. On the one hand, the election of Mary Robinson was seen to reflect both 'the symbolic revolution of women . . . in the teeth of macho resistance' and the crossing of 'the threshold of a new pluralist Ireland'. On the other hand, as several of the most seasoned campaigners of Fianna Fail were quoted as saying, the campaign was 'the bitterest campaign ever waged in this country'. Brian Lenihan said he had been 'witch-hunted'. His wife Ann said, 'they talk of betrayal', but she called it 'a crucifixion . . . for two weeks they crucified us from every corner'. The most obvious feature common to all sides involved in the campaign appeared to be the sudden eruption of what Edelman calls 'political arousal', which is essentially to do with intense emotions associated with certain political perceptions (Edelman 1971: ch. 1). I will return to this point below.

So, depending on one's perspective, what went so terribly wrong – or so unexpectedly right? The initial hypothesis presented in this research was that the presidential election campaign was primarily about change in political culture. But *exactly* what kind of change? Conventional political scientific tools were found to be inappropriate to answer this question. Close scrutiny of the academic literature on the subject revealed the validity of Cohen's point: conventional accounts of political events are essentially descriptions of only the political power game, and as such do not provide the tools to analyse the dynamics of cultural change, which is at source based on feelings and perceptions (Cohen 1985).

Accordingly, the search for a more relevant method of analysis has led me to hermeneutics, as advocated by Paul Ricoeur in particular (Ricoeur 1974, 1989). Hermeneutics was chosen because within it there appears to be space to examine the *meaning* of social facts. According to Edelman, the interpretation of meaning is different from the examination of information and facts, and the former is frequently incompatible with the latter. Meaning is associated with the symbolic order of things, although it necessarily uses empirical facts in its initial terms of reference. It is political perceptions that beget the emotion called political arousal. Political arousal therefore – a most unexpected characteristic exhibited during the last stages of the Irish presidential campaign – is created not by the 'facts' of a political event, but by how the facts are 'read' by different social and political groups. This raises the following questions. What political associations, significations or values were attached to the 'facts' surrounding Brian Lenihan and Mary Robinson's campaign? How was it that these 'facts' greatly disturbed, or further entrenched, previously internalised symbolic understandings of society?

Representation

Before I answer this complicated question a special caveat must be entered at this point. I make no claim that those interviewed for this research project are statistically representative of some larger population. That is not the point. I do claim, however, that any small group of subjects within a particular culture can legitimately be said to reflect or intimate the most deep-seated mental structures existing in some larger population of subjects making up that culture. In a sense, deep structures of thought are almost – but not quite – independent of individual thought; they are in large measure shaped by dominant historical cultural value systems. Along the same lines as Habermas, I view the 'narrative' – which I explain below – as a technique suited for interpretation generally. This is because we can legitimately 'abstract' from individual case histories if the 'action' within the narrative can be taken out of context and transferred to other life situations (Habermas 1979). I will show how the most dominant model, which I outline below – the 'politics of the fox' – may be abstracted in such a way.

In sum, and to reiterate Dryzek's and Berejikian's point as well, a small set of discourses has the capacity to generate and confirm a valid representation of a narrative existing within a larger population (Dryzek and Berejikian 1993). This is the kind of representation in which I am interested. Furthermore, the specific narrative technique I employ – intensive interviewing – accepts what conventional projects like to deny: the importance of subjective or individual opinion. This has proved to be crucial, for hermeneutics fully accepts that narrative analysis, including analysis based on intensive interviewing, is 'shot through with evaluation' (Bernstein 1976: 63). It is precisely the need to generalise or 'objectify' these evaluations that adds both depth and interest to the understanding of socio-political narratives.

METHODOLOGY

The basic premise of the linguistic and hermeneutic disciplines is that to speak of narrative is also to speak of culture. On a conceptual level, narrative is considered to be a metacode, a human universal on the basis of which messages about the nature of a shared cultural reality can be transmitted. In other words, by listening to people's stories, we may come to understand the reality of people's cultures. The hermeneutic project in particular is concerned with the primacy of the symbol, through which meaning emerges as indirect, mediated, enigmatic, complex and multiform (Ricoeur 1974, 1989).

In my overall project this means that retrieving thought from symbol is a 'method' for understanding some aspects of Irish political culture. This is to say that in an election campaign, in particular, a political action or statement, no matter how routine, will have a symbolic aspect if individuals or groups wish to bestow it with such significance (Cohen 1985: 42). Hence the need for a 'long detour' (as Ricoeur might say) through political thought systems and critical academic literature as a way of getting to symbols that are not immediately evident.

On a practical level, as noted above, the method of intensive interviewing was deployed. Intensive interviewing has the capacity to meet Ricoeur's two 'demands' of hermeneutic interpretation: 'distanciation' and 'appropriation'. It is beyond the remit of this chapter to dwell on the philosophy of social science involved in the explanation of these abstract concepts. It is sufficient to say that intensive interviewing allows narrators to tell their story in their own way and with very little interruption. This also means that the narrators will tend to create 'variables' peculiar to their own world-view, which in turn lends itself to a 'truer' representation. Although no details are provided in this chapter, the creation of a person's own variables is crucial in getting to the heart of symbolism.

Since cultural change and the presidential election campaign seem to be so intertwined, it was decided, as a starting point, to interview one member from each of the political parties that had actively campaigned during that campaign. Observing, albeit at a cursory level, that issues of gender, the family and the public behaviour of politicians had become associated with the two main candidates, it was decided to broaden the narrative base and include prominent one-issue groups. Accordingly, three narrators from the socially conservative lobby who see themselves as 'pro-family', and are usually known as 'pro-life' groups, and three of their opposites, from the 'pro-choice' groups, were included in the study. All told, eleven participants gave generously of their time for two interviews, each of approximately ninety minutes' duration. Twenty-three statements were taken from newspapers concerning the campaign and President Robinson's subsequent presidential activities up to September 1993. The narrators were asked to comment on any or all of the statements.

The second interview concentrated on two particular political issues that seemed to preoccupy and to be problematic for all the narrators in the first interviews. The first issue was that of political favouritism as a political norm. This phenomenon (in Hiberno-English) is commonly known as 'strokes', and the character who 'strokes' is usually referred to, positively, as 'the cute hoor' or more negatively, 'the major stroker'. The second issue concerned a politics of sexuality and the relevance of private life to political life. With hindsight, it was unnecessary to have interviewed three narrators from the 'pro-life' and 'pro-choice' groups each, as the 'pro-life' group members turned out to share identical thought systems, and the differences within the pro-choice group were not of a sufficiently fundamental nature to merit separate discussion. Inadvertently, I seem to have supported Dryzek and Berejikian's point: one 'soon get[s] to a point where adding individuals to the study does not yield any new information' (Dryzek and Berejikian 1993: 52).

Structuralist tools

Ricoeur, despite some criticisms, always suggests that structuralism is a method whereby the metacode of the narrative – and hence the culture – may be examined; it is an essential 'moment' in the process of interpretation. My investigation into structuralism as a methodology suggested a combination of the following structuralist analytical tools: (a) themes or oppositions, (b) philosophical metaphor, (c) transformations, and (d) binary opposites. This chapter focuses primarily on themes or oppositions.

The notion of using themes as an analytical tool caters for the idea that life is structured in terms of opposites or opposing themes which are always either positively or negatively charged. Themes, therefore, will always assign elements of the narrative to a general function of signification. The true significance of themes or oppositions are the assumptions that lie behind them. The problem of thematic extrapolation is thus very closely related to that of symbolic reading: by what 'informal logic' (Geertz 1975) or 'deep structure' (Chatman 1978) can we generalise from object or event – or candidate – and make it signify? The logic of symbolic recuperation, where causal connections are absent, is a rule-governed process employing incompatible antitheses as a formal device. If a narrative presents two items – characters, situations, events or beliefs – in a way that suggests opposition, then a whole space and variation is opened to the reader (Culler 1975). Lévi-Strauss has argued, for instance, that the words 'sun' and 'moon' cannot be used to signify anything in themselves, but put into opposition, there are no limits to the other contrasts that they might express (Lévi-Strauss 1963). In short, at their most basic level, political themes express the relation of an individual to the political world and to her/himself.

Political metaphors represent a vision of reality that underlies the entire body of political thought and is a most useful tool for highlighting tensions in thought systems. It is from here also that one can understand the deep structure of thought within any model of politics. In my project, by far the most dominant metaphor was that of war/death and explosive conflict. I refer to it briefly below.

'Transformations' signify a change in the dynamics of power and are thus important for any analysis of politics. 'Binary opposites' are really themes at their most basic level. The most fundamental source or terms of reference towards which interpretation moves is the body, so binary opposites will usually have a bodily reference, e.g. male versus female. To make the body the centre of the symbolic field, however, is only to say that it is an image of the force which ultimately subjugates other meanings. The most general thematic connection between consciousness and its objects, which falls also within the domain of the body, is that of happiness and unhappiness. This basic 'diffraction of desire', as Foucault calls it, is well reflected in the model of politics of those interviewed (Culler 1975; Foucault 1972c). I begin the first stage of my analysis with a description of a model of politics that I have called the 'politics of the fox'.

THREE MODELS OF POLITICS

The politics of the fox

In a moment I will justify why this model can be called the 'politics of the fox'. But first, I wish to highlight the main features of one particular narrator. The 'politics of the fox' is expressed as a positive model of politics by one narrator only, whom I call Raymond. It is the most important model of politics represented in this research, because its major theme, the successful and persistent *acquisition of power* for the sake of power only, is everyone else's major negative theme or antagonist. Raymond refers to and identifies with the largest political party in the country. Thus this model must have significant representative value. As with the other two models of politics, the following quotations are taken from two transcribed interviews that Raymond gave.

Unlike the other models, Raymond's model of politics has just one clear dominant theme – gaining and retaining power – and this is what politics is all about. He says 'your first objective is to get yourself elected'. Following this, pragmatism for Raymond is an important feature in his model of politics: 'there has to be a lot of pragmatism as distinct from principles in my party', because 'principles don't often get you elected'. Although unimportant for Raymond, principles intertwine with what was referred to above as 'strokes': his party's 'principles are basically pandering to capitalism, some elements of the farming community and a lot of middle-class people'. Once you do that, 'everything else will be OK'. For Raymond, 'strokes' seem to have other dimensions also: 'Politicians always favour their supporters . . . I don't think that impinges on the integrity of the political system.' Despite Raymond's party's history of phone-tapping, the political favouritism that became evident in the Beef Tribunal and the Telecom scandals, for instance, he is sufficiently comfortable with the notion of 'strokes' that he can say, 'while there may be incidents that point to dishonesty they are not an enormous magnitude'. In other words, Raymond can easily justify the notion that political integrity does not conflict with 'strokes' or pragmatism.

Furthermore, pragmatism seems sufficiently deeply embedded in Raymond's thought system that he can easily assume values that are perhaps contrary to his own. During the EU election campaign (June 1993) – seen as a 'bit of a gravy train' – it became necessary for his party to 'prompt liberalism' by running a surprise and explicitly liberal candidate in a liberal constituency. Raymond justifies this 'parachuting' by his traditionally conservative party on the grounds that 'sometimes you are better to follow the country's agenda as distinct from trying to lead the agenda [and] once you see there is public acceptance you can then take the lead and run with them'. Thus it is easy for Raymond to conform to different value systems if the acquisition of power is involved.

By the same token, it is difficult to assess Raymond's own value or thought system. His positions on feminism and homosexuality, however, are revealing. Feminism is not perceived to be a threat to society, 'because it gives men more freedom'. Not only is Raymond genuinely unaware of some or all institutionalised gender oppression, despite his relative youth (he is in his thirties), but he seems to understand feminism as providing only men with freedom. On the issue of homosexuality, Raymond believes that the government politician publicly revealed to have been in a place of sexual exploitation should have resigned. On the one hand, Raymond recognises the pragmatism of the government's response, saying, 'Given the liberal agenda in place at the moment, the coalition couldn't be seen to sack him . . . if his misdemeanour had been more socially acceptable he would have had to go.' On the other hand, and despite this recognition, Raymond believes that the politician in question should have resigned, because his activities were 'bordering on illegality, and he had . . . [consistently] ignored police warnings'. Since we know that principles do not feature in Raymond's model of politics, and public scandals attributable to his party are still considered to be 'within an honest framework', we may ask why something only 'bordering' on illegality is worth the potential loss of power. It is highly likely that Raymond does not view homosexuals in the same way as heterosexuals in terms of sexual equality.

In short, Raymond's model of politics is concerned primarily with the acquisition of power and the means by which to achieve this: pragmatism and 'strokes'. He has no time for principles. His own value system is probably socially conservative; he does not identify with feminism in the least, and his references to homosexuality are the only instances in which pragmatism comes off second-best. The question of political integrity or accountability does not arise.

This type of political behaviour is strikingly like Hanna Pitkin's image of 'foxy' behaviour, which she sees as prevalent in all Machiavelli's writings. In her book, *Fortune is a Woman*, Pitkin shows how Machiavelli's writing is dominated by three differing and widely contrasting symbolic images: the citizen, the founder and the fox. The image of interest here is the fox and its political behaviour. At the end of this chapter I will attempt to show that 'foxy' action has definite consequences for equality and democracy within Irish political culture. For the moment, though, I will only introduce the idea that the fox, according to Pitkin, is like Raymond, in that he is always a realist. He takes the world as it really is, whereas the fox can 'justify morally what would otherwise be unjust and can justify pragmatically what would otherwise be imprudent' (Pitkin 1987: 168). For the fox, political realism always means that 'ideals and principles can only be shams to deceive the gullible' (Pitkin 1987: 36, 95). There are other things to be said in relation to Raymond's model of politics, but I will delay that discussion until I can show what the other models of politics have to say about Raymond's 'foxy' model.

My understanding is that Raymond's model of politics seems to align itself fairly easily with the image of the fox, as interpreted by Hanna Pitkin, and that this behaviour is important for traditional political cultures, such as the one in Ireland. The next two models of politics will indicate that all narrators see Raymond's model of politics as it existed during the time of interviewing, and as it is reflected in the workings of the coalition government of 1993, as corrupt or, at the very least, undemocratic. This is what all, except Raymond, have called the existence of 'a serious crisis of democracy'. Observe that Pitkin's interpretation is that Machiavelli's entire thesis is a critique of the city of Florence, arguing that it has been destroyed by political corruption under the Medici family (Machiavelli 1970a; Pitkin 1987).

The politics of containment

The second model of politics is represented in what are usually termed the 'pro-life' groups. For the purposes of discussion within this model of politics, homosexuals are treated politically as belonging with women and within the category of the 'feminine', because the 'politics of containment' defines them both with this in common: they are to be negated or consigned to the private sphere. There are three narrators to this group: James, Brian and Nellie. Three main themes run through this model. The first theme concerns religious values. Political values should be derived from religious values or, as Brian puts it, 'fundamental law' is 'divinely sanctioned'. The second theme is to do with superior men. Men are better equipped to be leaders and to work, as men tend to be naturally 'more aggressive' and 'competitive', and women tend to be better at 'nurturing' and 'caring'; 'reverse discrimination', for instance, is 'unjust because you will not get the quality there'. The third theme – the primary function of politics – is encapsulated well by Brian: 'a lot of politics is containment, holding the lid on something . . . it's containing situations that are always threatening to get out of hand and putting lids on'. Furthermore, there are negative themes: first, working women – if women work, society turns out to be chaotic (I will say more on this shortly). The second negative theme relates to male role models: referring to unmarried mothers, this view says that children without male role models grow up in chaos and perpetuate an explosive type of society (James). The third negative theme relates to 'isms': the present government and 'all the isms' (feminism, liberalism, socialism, etc.), so it is said, encourage this destruction of society ultimately through the notion of sexual freedom; they totally misunderstand human nature. Ideally, political society should instil order into this present chaos; chaos should be contained. Some of the ways to do this are to insist on no-divorce and no-abortion policies.

It is necessary to look closely at this notion of social destruction and its connection to the notion of working women. This turns out to be what I see as an over-concern with sexual freedom or what the literature refers to as the 'passions'. According to the 'politics of containment' model, women in the workplace cause society to 'self-destruct' and 'children to run riot all over the place' (Nellie). This chaos is due, at least in part, to 'the 1960s sexual revolution' (Brian); the notion 'that today anything goes' (Nellie); we are now 'part of an amoral society where lack of traditional male role models have created floating barbarians without culture'. 'Unattached males with psychiatric problems' liaise with females who are 'non-achievers everywhere' (James). In other words, sexual freedom resulting from feminism and liberalism, in particular, causes what James calls a 'nitroglycerine problem' for society. In short, 'loose' sexual passions cause society to self-destruct.

The solutions to this problem, however, give the passions a different emphasis; they are directed solely towards removing women from the workplace. The political solution is no-divorce, because marriage for life – meaning women remaining at home – provides stability for 'men with short fuses'. The dominant positive themes suggest that the policies associated with the 'politics of containment' are ultimately directed to advantage men by keeping women out of the workplace. All narrators, for instance, had no solution or any answer to the demographic feature of smaller families, and the idea of reverse discrimination – a policy that might help women return to work – was viewed as 'unjust'. Furthermore, it is significant that 'technical junk', as James puts it (meaning hoovers and washing machines), is viewed not as a freedom but as a problem: 'I don't know what women can do now that they have less housework to do' (Brian). Nellie, the only woman in the group, was content with the notion that child-rearing, voluntary work and caring for ageing parents were the only activities suitable for women. In short, solutions to the thing that is destroying society – the passions – tend to focus on women generally; they are to remain outside the workplace.

My next section below applies certain political theories to this model of politics. In particular, I want to draw some similarities between particular aspects of Aquinas's thought and the 'politics of containment'. For this model of politics, everything should be derived from laws which are 'divinely sanctioned' (Brian). In other words, the Catholic ethos should dominate the polis. Similarly, Aquinas argues the importance of the polis as a teleological end, and thus he sees that the world of public action becomes a positive expression of our divine creation (Aquinas 1922). In other words, divine or natural law, or 'fundamental law' (Brian), gives rise to the human laws of the political community. Perhaps this is why, since 'the core of democracy is based on fundamental law' (Brian), a policy of no-divorce and no-abortion, also essential for the 'common good', can be said to be derived from something similar to Aquinas's notion of 'human reason', or aligning this with Brian's phrase, 'common-sense observation'. No-divorce and no-abortion, stemming ultimately from God's law, can thus be seen to be good for society. From this perspective, these policies can be argued to be democratic. Presumably this is also why this model of politics easily and frequently refers to laws that narrators do not like, such as the decriminalisation bill on homosexuality passed in 1993, as 'objectively evil'. This latter characterisation is peculiar to the 'politics of containment'.

It would seem that the thought system of this model may be aligned with other aspects of Aquinas's political philosophy also. Remembering that all narrators sincerely believe that their model of politics is based on the principle of equality (what James calls 'the principle of unconditional preciousness') and bearing in mind this model's emphasis on religious values, we note that Aquinas's theology moves beyond the imperfection of a being on earth, while also making distinctive claims for equality. In 'the order of salvation' that 'is beyond sexual distinction', men and women are treated equally (Aquinas 1922: 289). In other words, Aquinas posited an order in which men and women, no longer being limited by their bodies, could equally get to Heaven. There is thus an abstract kind of equality there: all souls have the same end (Saxonhouse 1985: 144–50).

It is very likely that views such as 'women are suited to nurturing only' and 'homosexuals are not fit to take up public life' are derived by the political philosophy of the 'politics of containment' from a theology such as this one. If one bears in mind the influence of Aquinas on Roman Catholic thought in general and the fact that Ireland is predominantly a Catholic country, the presence of this model of politics as an aspect of Irish political culture is hardly surprising.

In relation to equality, two other themes running through the 'politics of containment' markedly resemble certain aspects of Aquinas's naturalising and hierarchical model of society. This latter model entertains the notion that man's soul and thus his capacity for abstract reason is superior to what Aristotle, Aquinas's philosophical exemplar, called the 'misbegotten' male, i.e. woman (Aristotle 1992). Woman's sole capacity is for a specific type of practical reasoning, and her primary function in life, procreation, necessitates her exclusion from the polis. Man must therefore rule 'misbegotten' woman. Second, we saw that woman, although passive and inferior, somehow has the power to render society chaotic. Aquinas also saw that 'Women, through being unstable of reason, are easily led so they follow their passions readily' (Aquinas 1922:

173). For Aquinas and the 'containment' model then, the solution to this problem is similar: the adherence to 'natural' hierarchy and containment of the passions – in other words, the 'boiling pots' solution.

This teleological and naturalising principle of equality may be justifiable in terms of abstract equality. However, although men and women may be deemed equal at this abstract, transcendental level, it is clear that in the here and now, women should not only be denied equal political rights and employment opportunities but should also be constrained more severely than men, because they possess dangerous powers. Following Ricoeur's idea of metaphor, the dominant philosophical metaphor deep within the 'politics of containment' suggests that behind the masculine world of power, politics and work – the polis – there lurks a deep and complex image of feminine power. Passive, unintelligent misbegotten women possess mysterious and dangerous 'nitroglycerine' powers. This image also contains the idea that women, because they are dominated by their emotions rather than by their reason, are inferior. I call this complex image the 'nitroglycerine confusion', and I suggest that this 'confusion' is problematic for any genuine concept of equality, no matter how abstract. I will refer to this 'confusion' again later.

This brings us to the liberal model of politics and the five narrators identified with the 'politics of wounded hearts': Killian, Rachel, Maria, Margerie and Michele.

The politics of wounded hearts

The two dominant themes or oppositions in this model are what the narrators call 'liberalism' and 'patriarchy'. I will provide theoretical justifications for these terms shortly, but for the moment I note that there are some particularities regarding modern liberalism that I cannot explore in this chapter. Suffice it to say that at all times the principles of liberalism or the liberal agenda are equated by the narrators with the principles of democracy or the democratic project.

Liberalism can be subdivided into two dominant themes: 'sexual equality' and 'transparent democracy'. Patriarchy may be subdivided likewise: 'covert action' and 'institutionalised sexual oppression'. As a direct antithesis to 'covert action' in patriarchy, liberalism offers 'transparent democracy', and to 'institutionalised sexual oppression' in partriarchy, liberalism offers 'sexual equality'.

We begin with the positive theme of 'transparent democracy'. This concentrates in particular on the sub-theme 'inclusive democracy', thus rejecting Raymond's model of politics, because 'those on the margins haven't the slightest chance of becoming part of [our] culture' (Rachel). The positive theme of 'transparent democracy' acknowledges the effects of poverty, for example, as a dynamic of social conditioning which may lead to particular types of alienated action: 'these are forces that propel people inexorably into a life of crime and this is clearly an indictment of how we organise our society' (Rachel). As a result, rehabilitation, for example, is given priority in relation to current political issues, e.g. prisoners: 'one of the worst economies of the state is cutting down on social workers and its manned officers. I would much rather ten social workers than ten prison officers' (Michele). It is clear that the solutions by the 'politics of wounded hearts' to minority problems in general are fundamentally different from the more managerial and pragmatic solutions characteristic of patriarchal systems. The Irish state is seen as failing in its obligation to represent minorities or the marginalised. The primacy of political obligation relative to the recognition of rights is of crucial importance here, and it is regularly ignored by Irish politicians.

Not surprisingly, President Robinson is seen to represent democracy at its working best, because her political actions recognise everyone as equal regardless of social deprivation, differing intelligence or any other distinctive characteristic. She is seen as a 'flag' for genuine democracy (Michele). All narrators within this model believe that her election 'has forced us to confront difficult issues' (Killian), or 'she has revealed us to ourselves' (Rachel). As an extension of this theme, the 'wounded hearts' is the only model of politics that responds positively to the notion that political power ought to be devolved to a considerable degree to community groups. This particular model of politics sees this as an essential liberal principle and something 'acted out' by President Robinson's politics.

The need to respect differences and minorities, another sub-theme of 'transparent democracy', is a direct rebuke to what is perceived as the undemocratic political influence of Catholic institutions over the political process. This model strongly connects lack of respect for differences with the absence of political debate within the Irish political process. In short, all narrators see representative government as having two particular functions in this respect: to respect actively the rights of all, particularly the marginalised, and to institutionalise transparency through genuine political debate.

The other positive theme is 'sexual equality'. Women at all levels are seen to be equal to men, and homosexuals, in particular, deserve political acceptance. The decriminalisation bill concerning homosexuality was viewed as the principle of democracy 'truly at work'. Women have a right to work, and mothering is not and should not be seen to be all-consuming of a lifetime's work. Most of all, this model's notion of sexual equality seems to be a reaction to what I have called 'institutionalised sexual repression', explained below.

This negative theme is deduced from the fact that all the narrators see the political actors involved in 'covert action' – the Catholic Church and the pro-life groups – as overly concerned with the political 'control of female sexuality'. Furthermore these two latter groups exert undue influence over the political process. Margerie's remark is typical of the texts as a whole: 'No religious, especially male religious, has the right to tell a woman what to do with her own body.' Catholic views on homosexuality, for instance, are 'sheer poppycock . . . since you don't have to be a Catholic to be a homosexual, they don't make any sense' (Killian). Maria, in particular, is annoyed with what she sees as political hypocrisy in these patriarchal systems, especially the pro-life groups. She believes, for example, that there has been no official pro-life outcry concerning the disposal of frozen embryos by any of these institutions, and she concludes: 'If a right to life was *really* the issue, then there would be no real conflict.' In short, none of the above institutions is perceived to be democratic in any way, as they 'cannot ever accept opposing views' (Killian).

'Covert action' is the second negative theme. This refers to the process of democracy in general and to the coalition of 1993 in particular. The politics of 'Gombeenism', attributable solely to Raymond's party, 'has destroyed the political process in this country'. The image of Gombeenism or 'Gombeen politics' conveys a foolishness used to trick people into giving things away, despite their intentions to do otherwise. This particular political action – and the narrators provide several instances of Gombeen politics – is seen both as corrupt and as the essence of 'stroke' activity. It is devoid of all democratic principles, it is inherently elitist, and it has at its core political deception. It is patriarchal, inward-looking and anti-democratic, being concerned 'to sell their soul for the sake of power only' (Margerie). Because of the persistent quest for power and the consequent inward-looking perspective, this type of politics consistently ignores the political recognition of marginalised people: for example, 'travellers', prisoners, the unemployed and women.

In general terms, this system of 'covert action' is like Raymond's, except from a negative perspective; the image and political behaviour of the 'fox' are immediately evident. Therefore, before I discuss the liberalism behind the 'politics of wounded hearts', I need to say a few words about the remaining characteristics of the 'fox' and his political actions.

In the first model of politics, the 'politics of the fox', we have seen that the political action of the fox is, first, 'realistic', and second, totally unprincipled. A third characteristic of this 'foxy' politics, according to Pitkin, and, it would seem, particularly relevant to the 'politics of wounded hearts', is that of 'covert action'. I will show later that this type of action has serious consequences for democracy.

Covert action is referred to by Pitkin as 'furbo' activity and is associated with a 'skill in employing ruses that are usually . . . dishonest' (Pitkin 1987: 33). In a culture where 'furbo' activity is the norm, a man may be scrupulously moral in his relationships with his family and close friends, but yet take pride in his ability to cheat someone outside his own family, or better still, to defraud an organisation or public agency. The fear of being 'fesso', a victim, leads to an inordinate amount of mutual suspicion and makes amicable or honest relations almost impossible in the world of politics. The 'fox', this 'furbo', who for Pitkin has retreated from his emotions into his intellect, runs the show through his cleverness, through his reason. Most particularly, his pride and skill lie in his ability to deceive without being deceived himself.

In Machiavelli's texts the fox himself works behind the scenes, but in this project, only the fox's intentions are located there. A great deal of political behaviour therefore appears to be one thing while it is actually another. I am suggesting that the existence of 'strokes' and Gombeenism, a point that is confirmed by all narrators either implicitly or explicitly, can be aligned to this 'furbo' or deceptive activity. All narrators in this project see Raymond's party being involved in 'furbo' activity for the sake of retaining power. The 'wounded hearts' (as well as the 'politics of containment' narrators) see them as consummate deceivers and cynics, and it is clear that Gombeenism is akin to the notion of the fox's need 'to pretend idiocy' or 'play the fool' (Pitkin 1987: 13, 42).

Another dimension to this political deception is cynicism. This arises from 'scorn or disbelief' directed at the political system by those who have been outfoxed (Pitkin 1987: 22, 34). It is the most elemental characteristic of a political culture in which 'foxy' behaviour is the political norm, and it is remarkable how frequently this concept arises, quite unsolicited, in the texts of all narrators in this entire project. Cynicism, as Rachel says, is 'the enemy of democracy', and all narrators believe that Irish politicians are the established face of cynicism. In particular, the largest political party in Irish politics exemplifies this cynicism. Not surprisingly, as individuals, they admit to being extremely cynical about the democratic process themselves. In short (apart from Raymond), all narrators see a persistent 'crisis in Irish democracy' as a result of this cynicism. At this point it is worth noting that, as with Pitkin's cynical fox, it is obvious from Raymond himself that he is deeply unconscious of the fact that his own political outlook is cynical.

In short, 'foxy' behaviour or 'covert action' has 'killed off democracy' by corrupt 'strokes', by the 'art of hidden politics'. Much of what the 'fox' (Raymond) says of his own political party tends to reinforce this view, although he would not see it that way. The important point here is not that the political actions of the largest political party resemble Machiavelli's fox, which they do, but that such political behaviour is devoid of all mutuality. In other words, 'foxes' make poor citizens.

We now look briefly at some elements of liberalism to see if they can be aligned to the 'politics of the wounded hearts' model. At an abstract level, this model of politics, vigorously reacting to the 'dictates' of patriarchy, may be considered liberal because, like Locke, for instance, all narrators reject the view that some men have an inherent and natural right to govern others. Similar to this Lockean theme, the model in question also gives a prominent place to the consent of the governed as a means to ensure a balance between might and right. The revolutionary core of liberalism – that every individual is at liberty to compete for autonomy and success through the exertion of their will – seems to be at the heart of this model also. Thus the individual is seen to be the possessor of rights, the determiner of values, and the judge of the political system of which she or he is part. Most of all, and ideally, the political process exists to realise those rights. It has a moral obligation to do so. This model also seems to align itself with the classical liberal conception of parliament as a place where national policy is settled by rational reflection, guided only by the public or general interest. According to Mill's line of thought in 'Of the liberty of thought and discussion', rational debate is at the core of representative government, where 'freedom of opinion and freedom of the expression of opinion' is a 'necessity to the mental well-being of mankind' (Mill 1980).

In sum, this model appears to have absorbed some of the ideas of liberalism, and typical of contemporary liberalism, at least, it reacts vigorously to patriarchy. There are, however, some problems concerning the abstract notion of equality and its implications for concrete realisation within the political system. This turns out to be quite complex and necessitates looking at what I call the 'wounded hearts' denial'.

'Wounded hearts' denial'

I want now to illustrate the argument that on a concrete level, or on the level of political action, the 'politics of wounded hearts' (somewhat understandably) is not always able to follow through on liberal ideas of equality. I argue that this creates problems somewhat similar to, though perhaps not quite as serious as, the problem of inequality that is created by the 'nitroglycerine confusion'. As a basic premise for my own argument here, it needs to be stated that I accept that Phoenix Park in Dublin becomes a place of inequality and homosexual exploitation at night-time.

One of this model's particular objections to 'foxy' covert action is that 'foxy' politicians are, as Margerie puts it, 'hypocrites' – they preach one thing and do another. The 'back to basics' policy in England, and politicians who have affairs and yet preach anti-divorce in this country, were frequently given as examples. For the 'wounded hearts', the theme of 'covert action' always incorporates themes of deception and political hypocrisy, and their model of 'transparent democracy' is a direct counter to this type of institutionalised deception. By their own liberal logic then, the government politician publicly revealed to have been seen and warned several times by the police to stay out of Phoenix Park ought to have resigned. First, he was repeatedly in a place where only sexual exploitation or inequality and presumed secrecy exists, even though, as Margerie says, 'he is passionate about equality'. Therefore his behaviour can be regarded as covert at least by association. Bearing in mind that the politician's homosexual actions in Phoenix Park are beyond consideration and of no interest in the argument presented here, yet the reaction to them by the above narrators is very important to their model of equality. So, even if it could be argued that his behaviour was solely private and personal and thus outside his public role, by this model's own criteria of political hypocrisy he is said to be found wanting: his private persona – associated with inequality/exploitation by being consistently in a place of inequality or exploitation despite warnings – contrasts greatly with his publicly stated abhorrence of all kinds of inequality. That is to say, in a sense he 'preached' equality and 'practised', at least by association, inequality. All narrators of this model, however, fully approved of the politician's party leader's refusal to ask for his resignation. It might also be argued that the solution to this particular political action represented 'foxy' deception – or at least an attempt at it: both the party leader and the politician in question denied any inappropriate involvement (by the politician), but at the same time he apologised profusely and said that he would not repeat such actions again – 'foxy' denial, perhaps.

The argument presented here is that a politics of sexuality (sexual equality), hitherto treated as *equal* to the theme 'transparent democracy', is given greater priority than the practice of 'transparent democracy'; and furthermore, an element of the major antagonistic theme, 'covert action', is now acceptable in order to achieve this priority. There is thus something of a paradoxical element to the argument. Although several narrators saw the politician as a 'lunatic' (Maria) or as 'having a death wish' (Margerie), when he went to Phoenix Park in the first place, no narrator saw that his/her own explicit defence of this activity as impinging on his/her own principles of liberal equality. There exists, therefore, a particular type of denial, the 'wounded hearts' denial'. I suggest that the model of 'transparent democracy' flounders under the weight of the 'wounded hearts' denial', because it is now allowed to incorporate an element of 'covert action', something that would be vehemently denied on a conscious level by the 'politics of the wounded hearts'.

From the narrators' discourse it is more than clear that the real reason for their (illiberal) support is that it 'was a legitimate protest against the stigma of his homosexual activity', against the forces of patriarchy and of fundamentalism. Even accepting this point entirely, I still think it can be argued that behind these realistic and strategic answers lie abstract and symbolic difficulties which have serious implications for the deep structure of this model's ideas on political equality without patriarchy. I will continue this point on a more general level in a moment. Right now, two other brief points need to be made.

First, it has already been stressed that this model's sense of natural equality stems from each individual's right to rule over her/himself and not to submit to another's rule except by consent. Both Hobbes and Locke justified equality in that there are no teleological or moral criteria according to which some self-moving bodies may be ranked above others (Hobbes 1968; Locke 1947). All are equal by virtue of each person's ability to assume power over another. Hobbes's claim to such basic psychology, in particular, avoids any image or symbolism of gender because he makes no mention of reproductive or sexual needs, therefore avoiding any suggestion of associated innate, mental or relevant physical–sexual needs. Sexual difference simply does not matter.

Throughout the discourses of the 'wounded hearts' model there is, surprisingly, a complete absence of sexual differentiation and a consequent need for central policies, such as nursery childcare support, adequate maternity (or paternity) leave and so on. In this sense, their most abstract principle of equality seems to concur with Hobbes's materialist equality, for there is nothing in Hobbes's principle that says that sexual difference should be a criterion for either inclusion or exclusion, since there is no symbolism of gender or of sexual orientation. The 'wounded hearts' denial' has shown, however, that sexual difference matters greatly. It has created a particular element or symbolism of gender or sexual orientation which was explained by the narrators in question as 'liberal compassion' and 'tolerance' but which is also associated with covert 'foxy' behaviour and patriarchy. Thus their abstract liberal principle of equality is thrown into jeopardy; it now has an image of gender or sexual orientation, and one that is essentially associated with both democratic tolerance *and* 'foxy' behaviour.

Second, the dominant metaphor of all narrators in this research is that of war, with defensive strategies and social destruction emphasised. In one way this is hardly surprising, as this, too, is patriarchal, hierarchical and based on domination. What is surprising, however, is that the 'wounded hearts' model, while consciously professing a passive terminology – mutuality, dialogue, transparency – subconsciously deploys war-like strategies when imagining a model of politics. So even if the 'wounded heart' paradox had not arisen, the paradoxical nature of a political thoughtsystem that 'talks' mutuality but 'thinks' war, is always going to be problematic.

So far, the 'politics of wounded hearts' has been seen to incorporate liberal tenets, and I have borrowed from Mill and Locke and finally from Hobbes. Most particularly, on a conscious level of thought, this model could be aligned with Hobbes's abstract model of equality: sexual differentiation was ignored, and thus there was no need for a particular symbolism. This model is also rights-based, and the narrators would claim an equal and liberal emphasis for both themes, 'transparent democracy' and 'sexual equality'. The 'wounded hearts' denial', however, highlights the peculiarity that not only is their category 'sexual equality' given greater political emphasis, despite claims to the contrary, but also it has enacted an aspect of 'covert action' in order to achieve this emphasis. Relative to political action, then, a particular symbolism of gender or sexual orientation was introduced, one that conveys the image of both democratic tolerance and anti-democratic covert action. The particular point to remember is that this element of covert action was treated as an action of equality, so a particular type of denial was needed. To add to this, the vision of reality that underlies this political thought, like the two patriarchal models previously discussed ('politics of the fox' and 'politics of containment'), is warlike and uncompromising.

In this chapter two models are patriarchal. In the 'politics of the fox', power is *the* patriarch, in the sense that it is the guiding force of all elitist decision-making and is explicitly without principles. Furthermore, those who abide by the dictates of power are primarily concerned with exercising a particular type of 'foxy' reason in order to achieve superiority. The 'politics of containment' is even more explicitly patriarchal, declaring that women – because of their nurturing ability and particular type of practical reason – are not fit for the polis. Men, because of their superior abstract reason, are more capable of making decisions on behalf of society. The important point here is this: accepting that patriarchy has always been associated with the male order of things, there is thus an explicit image or association of 'maleness' with superior types of reasoning within both models. The association between patriarchal maleness and 'foxy' reason is also recognised – and condemned – by the 'politics of wounded hearts'.

The 'wounded hearts' model incorporates several basic liberal tenets, in particular individual autonomy and a strong sense of political obligation. A specific image of equality – nurturing woman, who politically empowers and is exemplified by Mary Robinson, and, as they see it, is inherent in liberalism – is at the core of this latter abstract model of equality. However, both the 'nitroglycerine confusion' and the 'wounded hearts' denial' exhibit unintentional contradictions. On one hand, passive misbegotten woman has the power to destroy society (the 'nitroglycerine confusion'), and on the other hand, despite equal emphasis on the categories of 'sexual equality' and 'transparent democracy', an aspect of 'covert action' was deployed in order to prioritise 'sexual equality'. This in turn introduced a particular symbolism of gender – incorporating both tolerance and 'covert action' – which was not part of their consciously declared model of equality ('wounded heart's denial').

INTERPRETATIVE ANALYSIS

In a hermeneutic project one has to address some inevitable problems which arise, in the main, from the nature of structuralist methodology. The first problem, as noted already, is that of representation, to which I will refer briefly again in a moment. The second is a phenomenological problem: structuralist analysis is frequently accused of eliminating the relevant phenomena, consciousness or the subject which constitute or shape the narratives of those interviewed. The following section attempts to remedy these deficits, albeit in a limited way. I do this by focusing on psychoanalytic theory in order to 'understand' the two patriarchal models of politics in the hermeneutical sense. At the time of writing, an adequate literature review, which might have explained fully the cultural psychic perspective of the 'wounded hearts' model in the same psychoanalytic vein as the other two models, is proving difficult. I wish to understand more fully the mind-set of those who are vehemently anti-'fox', anti-'containment', yet deploy 'foxy' ruses while at the same time denying doing so. In particular, and added to this, the literature would have to explain why this model consistently 'thinks' and combines metaphors of damaged, battered and wounded hearts with metaphors of war and social destruction as one system of politics, while it 'talks' mutuality, open dialogue and so on, just as well. Despite this difficulty, I believe that comments from a feminist critique of the history of philosophy, particularly from Genevieve Lloyd, are a satisfactory way of explaining some elements of the 'wounded hearts' denial'. In the following section, I look at certain elements of psychoanalytic theory which may be aligned with the two models of patriarchy under discussion.

Traditional societies and psychoanalytic theory

In rigidly gender-separated or traditional societies, Slater, for instance, claims that certain socio-cultural patterns of behaviour develop which have direct consequences for political action, and thus for equality and democracy (Slater 1968). I am taking it as given that Ireland has been, at least up to very recently, legitimately considered a traditional country. In this section I wish to assess whether Ireland can be seen as traditional in the sense that Slater means it. Of interest here is Slater's hypothesis that traditional countries have a tendency to develop specific anti-democratic cultural projections or fantasies, and that one needs to understand the significance of those fantasies in order to understand the political culture in question (Slater 1968).

In *The Glory of Hera*, Slater re-works the Freudian Oedipal situation. He looks at the way that men experience relationships with women in their infancy by focusing on the cultural dominance of mothers in a traditional society. The reality of traditional societies is that women controlled, sometimes absolutely, the private sphere. This private dominance, paradoxically coupled with her lowly public status, ensured that her primary social requirement was to reproduce a heavy cultural valuation of masculinity in her male children. This social conditioning resulted in what Slater calls a classical 'double bind' in the male child: an over-concern for his masculinity due to lack of identification with a near-permanently absent father, and a fear of his mother's near-absolute power over him. In 'father-remote' families the male can only develop a sense of what is masculine through identification with fantasy-type and abstract cultural images of masculinity. As a result, males in a traditional society develop a tremendous personal stake in the stereotypically socially available gender definitions. One of these 'definitions' is that there is a distinct masculine realm that is superior to the feminine, and that they alone are admitted to it; yet they remain intensely ambivalent about female dominance or 'femaleness' in general. Added to this, Slater also suggests that what the psychology literature always refers to as the 'other' of the 'self' (meaning the feminine side of the male self) is likely to threaten the psychic integrity of individuals who have absorbed stereotypical cultural images of masculinity only. This is because 'self' or male images which are acquired through merely cultural means (because of near-permanently absent fathers) are always oversimplified, exaggerated, and ultimately unreal. That is to say, whoever is excessively ambivalent about femaleness seems to find it difficult to acknowledge the female 'other' inside the self. Part of the self that seems alien, dangerous and in conflict with the accepted self is likely to project its 'otherness' onto external groups. Ascribing the forbidden 'other' of the self to groups allows us to ascribe to those groups what we feel about the other parts of the self. This is one of the most common explanations of racism and homophobia, for instance. It is clear from the literature that gender-fixed or traditional societies tend to facilitate those projections as cultural phenomena (Slater 1968).

In sum, in traditional societies, male individuals, because of institutionalised gender division, have a tendency to develop stereotypical images of masculinity which also have repercussions for cultural feminine images. A cultivated psychic ambivalence towards the feminine causes male individuals to fear the 'other' within themselves. Aligning Slater's hypothesis to Irish culture, it can be seen how this psychic ambivalence towards women may also be culturally realised by notions of superior men, passive or inferior women and perhaps homophobia. Since this ambivalence as well as this stereotypical acquisition of masculinity may also have implications for 'foxy' political behaviour, I examine the political consequences arising from such 'private' actions.

The literature of modern social science, including Banfield, Almond and Verba, and Pitkin, claims that there are political actions peculiar to the type of traditional societies under discussion (Almond and Verba 1965; Banfield 1958). In general, the hypothesis is that political activity can be essentially privatised – that is, the actors are absorbed into their immediate and direct relationships, unable to perceive the larger whole, incapable of sustaining a public, political life. They are incapable of extending their relationships beyond the personal and face-to-face to the public, which is by definition impersonal, large-scale and remote. Those who take as their rule of life the maximisation of private advantage, who conceive of such advantage and who think in short-range terms without hope for a different future – such people make poor citizens. Feeling no positive connection between themselves and others outside their immediate circle, they do not perceive themselves as a part of an active or involved public. Each strives to win at the expense of others. Politics becomes a zero-sum game where whatever is gained by some must be lost by others; the only rational defence becomes the pre-emptive strike – to act like a 'fox', in other words. This activity may call forth great expenditure of energy and it ultimately forms standards of achievement that are culturally accepted as a system of politics, but which have nothing to do with democracy.

These points do seem relevant indeed to Irish political culture, as in Irish academic literature the phenomenon just mentioned is highly suggestive of what is usually called 'cute hoor' activity, 'parish pump politics' or 'clientism'. Conventional academic literature on Irish politics may well be referring to these two patriarchal models of political thought when they refer to the 'denial and cultural defence' aspect of Irish political culture. Bearing in mind that the 'politics of the fox' is based on self-interest only, and the 'containment' model seems hopelessly determined to live in 'an Ireland that is long since past' – a traditional society (Rachel) – they are, I suggest, immersed in a particular type of political denial. This denial may partially explain why issues such as the abortion and divorce debates of 1983 and 1986, for example, turn out to be 'nothing more than a mechanism which protects people against the necessity to confront change, and permits a politics of cultural defence which could ignore change' (Garvin 1988: 1–7).

In sum, it seems reasonable to suggest that a traditional society like Ireland may perpetuate cultural perspectives that facilitate both the notions of superior men and inferior women and so on, as well as encouraging self-centred and defensive ('foxy') political activity, which has little to do with democracy or equality. Thus the 'politics of the fox' and of 'containment' are merely two different strategies for coping with the same psychoanalytic problem of being male in a traditional society.

Therefore within Irish political culture the significance of the 'politics of the fox' and of 'containment' and the implications for genuine democracy are not to be underestimated. Bearing in mind that all the narrators view the 'politics of the fox' as a vision of party-political reality, and that they relate this to the largest political party with the largest single first-preference voting base, we may say that, as with Florentine politics in Machiavelli's time, the real problem of Irish democracy may be that this 'foxy' ideal has become a real 'character type', a way of life (Pitkin 1987: 54). The 'cute hoor' or the 'stroker' may well be the Irish equivalent of the Florentine fox.

The 'fox', and in our case the political system, are thus doubly disparaged: he and it can neither reflect citizenship, nor can he and the political system ever be truly democratic. Thinking along these lines, I believe, serves to increase the representative value of this project. I hope that it also provides a suitable direction for pursuing phenomenological understanding, and thus 'returning' to the narrative of Irish political culture.

I have argued, following Slater and Pitkin in particular, that the political behaviour attributable to the 'politics of the fox' and the 'politics of containment' are also strategies or political manifestations of a gender-fixed and traditional society. Perhaps it may also be argued that the 'politics of containment' is as 'foxy' as the 'fox' himself. Using the principle of equality as a fundamental law, this model of politics devises sophisticated arguments and policies that ultimately separate men from what they have learnt to fear most: feminine power and/or a 'feminine' self. In the guise of equality and democracy men remain safely 'protected' by reason and by maleness – and thus from their own unconscious fears. It is important for this project that 'foxy' reason, now attributable to two models of politics, excuses both from genuine democratic effort. This brings us to the last model under discussion, the 'politics of wounded hearts'.

Feminist critique and the 'politics of wounded hearts'

In this section I borrow heavily from a feminist critique of the history of philosophy. The general disinclination of the 'wounded hearts' model to absent itself from all aspects of 'covert action', despite claims to the contrary, or more specifically a particular denial, may be connected not only to practical if genuine 'obstacles' in Irish conservative society – such as a determination to make a statement against the forces of homophobia – but also to *conceptual* obstacles as well. In particular, I am referring to what Lloyd calls the symbolic weight of 'the maleness of Reason' (Lloyd 1993). In *The Man of Reason* Lloyd shows how, historically, our ideals of maleness and femaleness have been formed within structures of dominance, how ideals of rationality have been formulated with only male paradigms in mind, and last, how these male–female opposites ought not to be taken as straightforward descriptive principles of classification but as an expression of cultural values.

One explanation for the 'wounded hearts' denial', therefore, is that this model of politics has been conceptually formulated in relation to and differentiation from a male political norm only. Therefore we may say that the 'wounded hearts', while vigorously reacting to what they see as patriarchal norms, also lack alternative political concepts of equality. This model seems to have no other option but to define itself, at least partially, by these dominant political male norms. It could be argued that the basic tension within Irish political culture on a conceptual level is that the 'politics of wounded hearts' has immense difficulty in accommodating itself into a historical cultural ideal which has been defined in opposition to genuine political equality, in opposition to the 'politics of wounded hearts'.

CONCLUSION

On a concluding note, I observe that on one level the traditional and liberal thought systems presented here loosely represent the history of political thought world-wide. This has unfolded as an ongoing debate between those who insist on hierarchy and their opponents who espouse equality. Similar to these two general historical thought systems, and which, I suggest, also underlie the models of politics in this chapter, it may well be that there is perhaps a deeper universal consensus which presents the feminine, or what is coded as feminine, as antithetical to qualities of reason, and, if the 'nitroglycerine confusion' (or Aquinas) is to be taken seriously, to civilisation itself (Saxonhouse 1985; Lloyd 1993).

We have seen that 'the politics of the wounded heart' gives priority to free expression of political sexuality by borrowing back a distinctly patriarchal theme: 'covert action', in order to get 'feminine' sexuality politically accepted. An alignment here with Lloyd's pessimistic point concerning the overall history of philosophy might lead one to believe that, as she says, the 'feminine' is indeed constructed as that which must be dominated if politics – leaving equality aside – is to persist (Lloyd 1993). In the discourse of the narrators the 'covert action' under discussion was presented as synonymous with liberal 'compassion' and 'tolerance' for homosexuality, and as a just reaction to fundamentalist patriarchy in particular. Thus there may be an argument for the idea, whether we like it or not, that in the guise of transparency and equality, to re-work de Beauvoir's well-known phrase, 'democracy still dreams through the dreams of men; even if women are now doing that dreaming'. This is particularly so if one remembers that a dominant metaphor here is also that of war. As such, the uncomfortable aspect of this research indicates the validity of feminist literature on the subject, which argues that the 'maleness of reason' pervades even feminist thought systems (Bryson 1994).

On the more immediate level I have attempted to show that psychoanalytic theory suggests that psychic life has its political counterparts. This research project has identified some political counterparts to individual repression as manifested by traditionalism. This counterpart reflects a politics of domination – of 'foxy' behaviour, of 'containment', where a few make the rules by which others are forced to live. Political sublimation, on the other hand, may well have been realised by Mary Robinson as a working democratic ideal – an ideal whereby democracy caters for 'others', for minorities.

Finally, my own argument relating to both the 'nitroglycerine confusion' and the 'wounded hearts' denial' is this: because ideals are humanly made, leaving their care and maintenance to some transcendent power amounts to a serious failure of political responsibility by the 'politics of containment'. It is also an act of extreme 'foxy' deception. Yet precisely because political ideals promote a better life for human beings than 'foxy' pragmatism, the inability of the 'wounded hearts' to recognise the non-adherence of their own declared ideals is also a failure of political responsibility. In partial defence of this latter model of politics, however, their thought system – their specific pragmatic defence of 'alternative' sexuality – has developed inside the labyrinth of actual power and covert political practice. Within Irish political culture this is something of a remarkable achievement in itself. One of the real problems, of course, is that, conceptually speaking, actual power has not yet been 'feminised'. In other words, to date there appears to be no concept of power other than patriarchy in a direct system of governmental politics.

I will not offer such concepts of 'feminised' power here except to refer to the point with which I began: the election of Mary Robinson and its symbolic representative value. Beyond the politics of power, what else was the election about? Was the election of Mary Robinson a moment when cultural repression was replaced by sublimation? Was Irish political culture experiencing a 'rebirth', because at least for a short space of time, a moment perhaps, Irish political culture was no longer 'hung up' on traditionalism and the Catholic ethos? By electing a misbegotten female with obvious intelligence and an active sense of equality, Irish society perhaps looked to a future, to a recovery, some would say, of the public self, to a recovery of capacities previously hidden by cultural reification, to a recovery of the public self as the product of history and of those parts of that history that had been distorted or disguised. Rachel puts this much better with some interesting phrases: Mary Robinson's election was a recovery of the 'private pagan' self which challenged for the first time the 'public Catholic' Ireland, which she sees as a 'mere nineteenth-century convention'. Perhaps it was also a moment when Irish society recovered awareness of its stake in the public, and at the same time redefined the public in terms of justice, transparent politics and, above all, 'woman' as equal, as explicitly *un*misbegotten. As such, it has been said, we freed ourselves, however momentarily, to act effectively as a community instead of being deadlocked in factional strife or resentfully bound to the past in the form of political vengeance, suspicion and 'strokes'. If this is so, if a democratic ideal is consistently being realised by an Irish President – despite the 'luxury' of the absence of governmental power – then the democratic project is perhaps safer than this chapter initially seemed to suggest.

6 Mapping women, mapping the self
Representations of women in participation studies

Marja Keränen

At about 10 o'clock, the other observer was passed by 32 men and 68 women. Only three men and four women stopped to look at an advertisement. In addition, 12 men and 21 women noticed an ad but did not read it. One passenger car stopped, so that the people in it could get acquainted with the controversy between two political parties, represented on large boards.

(Pesonen 1965: 171)

INTRODUCTION

In the 1950s the importation of behavioural studies into Finnish political science established a new conceptual architecture. This opened up a new structure of questions to be asked in research. This genre became more influential than the actual number of studies would suggest.

The new genre opened up 'the individual level' as a field of study. For voting studies, 'getting nearer the individual' was seen as a new possibility. The search was for 'fluctuations in individual voters' opinions and possibilities for affecting them'. By interviewing voters it was now possible to discover 'the effects of the voters' characteristics and attitudes and of the environment on voting intentions and on the final voting decision' (Pesonen 1958a: 19).

In replacing earlier genres the rhetoric imported by behavioural studies was that of realism. Even the move 'nearer the individual' can be seen as a move in the direction of realism, getting nearer the referential, the 'true reality'. This was advanced with the help of survey techniques for interviewing voters. Reference to 'the real' empowered these texts and legitimated this research as true science.

However, reference to 'the real' also made the texts dialogical and multivocal; 'other voices' coming from the 'field' of study were presented in the texts by the author(s). Hence there is a possibility of tracing 'other voices' in the text and of analysing the dialogue between the referential and the author in the texts.

Getting into dialogue also implied a counter-tendency: the 'other voices' were transported into another language game, given new meanings by the author. This raises a question: are behaviourist studies using a new vocabulary and a new language that actually creates distance and 'oddifies' the everyday?

In this chapter, I will try to trace 'other voices' within certain texts drawn from the behaviourist genre. Just as the texts that I analyse re-textualise 'other voices' and orchestrate them into a multivocal textuality, so do I in my writing. I will be translating these texts into my own language for purposes of this discussion.

One of the 'characteristics of the individual' observed in these texts was gender. In or by means of behaviourism, representations of gender became visible in political science. In the new conceptual architecture, gender became visible by becoming one of the 'variables' determining political behaviour or political activity. A standard was established that put gender into analysis as a background variable, although this was not always followed through, and even less reflected upon.

What were the gender identities created? What were the representations? What meanings were given to gender? What values were attached to it? What do the representations tell us? This chapter begins by looking at what was said about women in behavioural studies and how the language actually worked.

Going further, I shall be asking how the discourse was organised and what the representation of women, the 'placing of women in the discourse', tells about the discourse itself. Turning the question inside out, by looking at the representations of gender, I also intend to pose questions about the conceptual architecture within which gender became visible.

With only slight exaggeration, the conclusion of the behaviourist studies can be stated as 'women are passive in politics'. This conclusion can be seen as a 'fact' produced by behaviourist discourse in a disciplinary context. The findings of behaviourist studies on gender can be summarised as: 'Men were more interested in politics, more exposed to the mass media, offered more numerous political opinions and were more often opinion leaders than women' (Pesonen 1960a: 6). To this 'finding' behaviourists added that women were also 'more conservative' than men (Pesonen 1960a: 8; Rantala 1956).

The questions that I ask in this chapter are the following. What is the rhetorical organisation of the 'fact' that 'women are passive in politics'? How was the 'fact' produced? How did the 'fact' gain its status as such? How did it become credible?

The 'data' under analysis here have a somewhat marginal character in political science literature. It should be borne in mind that the genre of behavioural studies in itself is only one part of the literature on political science in the 1950s and 1960s. And even within behavioural studies, there is no single work explicitly on gender.

Furthermore, this chapter is a radically reduced version of a larger manuscript and therefore draws on a limited number of texts within the behavioural genre. After presenting some 'contexts', the chapter then concentrates on texts by Pertti Pesonen. Pesonen's work has been chosen because of a necessity to limit the field of study. However, it does not differ radically from what was written (or indeed what could be written) within the genre by other authors. In any case Pesonen was a central figure within the genre. And within Pesonen's *oeuvre*, the question of gender is actually a very central one. It is discussed in his two main monographs, *Student Voters in the Election of Presidential Electors* (1958a) and *A Mandate from the People* (1965). Before attending to the principal subject of the chapter, however, I will present some counter-, con- or pre-texts in order to frame my discussion.

A CONTEXT

The first Finnish behavioural studies were published in 1956. From the point of view of this chapter, however, I will treat them as contextual or pre-textual. The first one, the contextual case, is a map without people. The data used were official election statistics, and the unit of analysis was geographical area rather than individuals. Jaakko Nousiainen's dissertation *Communism in the Province of Kuopio* (1956) is an ecological analysis modelled after French studies. It analyses the support of the Communist movement in two neighbouring electoral areas consisting of fifty-three communes or municipalities.

The work represents a conceptual architecture that does not actually include individuals, so there appears to be no gender. Although women's and men's voting behaviour is not analysed, the differences between voting behaviour in the neighbouring municipalities of Vehmersalmi, Riistavesi and Siilinjärvi are thoroughly analysed. The soil, climate and natural environment of Kuopio province are analysed in great detail (Nousiainen 1956: 127, 114).

The architecture of political regionalism was followed by other works and produced a vocabulary of 'political behavioural areas' and 'political climate areas' (Nousiainen 1958; also Burman 1957; Lehto 1959). The concepts were drawn from geography, or even biology. Not only the metaphors of atmospheres and changing weather became common, but also the perspectives of anthropology, cultural studies and cultural traditions were invoked (Nousiainen 1960: 123–38; Rantala 1962).

Nowadays the conceptual map of political regionalism has a certain fascination. Why, indeed, should individuals be relevant in political topographies? When did individuals actually become relevant units in politics? Why could not the metaphors of climate and nature be used as well as the ones we are currently using that appear normal to us today?

A PRE-TEXT: GENDER DIFFERENCES IN VOTING

The pre-textual case, also from 1956, is Erik Allardt's dissertation 'Social structure and political activity 1945–1954' (see also Allardt and Bruun 1956). Like Nousiainen's study it was based on analysing voting statistics. Gender was easily drawn from statistics, so the work also gives information about the voting percentages of men and women. The pre-text presents a map based on voting statistics, including gender.

For the period 1945–1954, the difference between the voting percentages for men and women for the whole country was found to be about 5 per cent (Allardt 1956: 125). However, after elaborating the results from Helsinki with respect to age and marital status and then standardising the effect of these intervening variables, it turned out that gender difference diminished to a very small value. Elaborated this way, the percentage for men was 76.9 per cent and for women 76.2 per cent (Allardt 1956: 128–30). The text concludes: 'It would be interesting to know to what extent the greater voting passivity among women reported in other studies can be traced in a similar way back to demographic factors' (Allardt 1956: 130).

Although this work is treated as contextual (which is also in accord with the institutional criteria applied in my work – it comes from sociology and not political science), it must, however, be counted as a relevant intertext, as common knowledge in the scientific community of the time, being the first and foremost work in the area. Therefore I call it pre-textual. This pre-text, based on voting statistics, seems to indicate that no gender difference existed in political activity.

'FINDING' A GENDER DIFFERENCE, MEETING THE FINNISH 'REALITY': THE RHETORIC OF MEASURING POLITICAL ACTIVITY

However, mapping individuals was more effectively done by using new survey methods for gathering interview data. Pertti Pesonen's work has been influential in introducing this type of study into Finnish political science. The following discussion will be based on his texts. I will look at the relationship between voting (voting statistics) and political activity (interview data), as it appears in his work.

When comparing the voting percentages of women and men in the larger monographs of Pesonen (1958a and 1965), the result – equal voting percentages – is actually confirmed. Pesonen, studying a student population in the presidential elections of 1956, reported the following voting percentages: men – 88.6 per cent, women – 89.1 per cent. From this, he draws the following conclusion: 'In Helsinki female students voted as actively as men did' (1958a: 136–7).

Pesonen's later study (1965: 242) of the parliamentary elections of 1958 reported the following voting percentages:

- Tampere: men – 82.4 per cent, women – 73.9 per cent;
- Korpilahti: men – 79.6 per cent, women – 70.1 per cent.

Whether the difference would have disappeared when controlled with some other intervening variable, we do not know.

A political scientist does not control the production of voting statistics, whereas there is considerably greater freedom in defining 'political participation' with the help of survey methods. Interestingly, a clearly defined gender difference was 'found' in political participation.

To illustrate this, I will construct a narrative that follows the structure of reporting for an empirical study. How were women represented? How was the 'fact' of women's passivity established in relation to 'reality' in Finland?

Introducing difference

What are the various ways of introducing gender to the reader, i.e. ways of representing the gender difference? How is gender difference framed? How does a text get a discussion of gender difference started?

Gender difference in political activity is constantly represented in relation to comparable results abroad. In Pesonen's work it is introduced as 'observations on Anglo-Saxon voters' (1958a: 23–31), and stated as hypotheses for the study: 'It is generally stated, that women take part in elections relatively weakly/unenthusiastically in comparison to men. . . . Even in general, women have been found more conservative than men. . . . Also in England, it has been found' (Pesonen 1965: 31). The most specific version is: 'In the USA and Great Britain, it has been stated . . . ' (1958a: 72–3).

Located between Anglo-American participation studies and 'Finnish reality', how does the argument advance? 'It has been commonly stated that women take part in elections relatively less enthusiastically than men. That is how it has been even in Finland in all national elections after women got the vote over a half-century ago' (Pesonen 1958a: 27). But the text goes on:

> Even in the elections of 1956 there was a difference. The voting percentage of men was 76.1% and of women 71.0%. It should, however, be particularly noted that in the electoral district of Helsinki the difference had diminished almost to non-existence: 75.6% of men and 75.2% of women voted. Even in general, the voting frequencies of men and women were less different in cities than in the countryside.
>
> (Pesonen 1958a: 57)

As the text draws attention to the possibility of variation and to 'less different' political activity, we might expect this to be a good starting point for empirical research. But no! The difference was shown to be international. It was simply imported into the hypotheses of these Finnish studies. In fact, no Finnish study ever set out to find local variations or suggested the possibility of results that differed from the 'international law' of women's passivity. The 'finding' of women's passivity was imported as a universal, and it was thus generalised over space. This 'general observation' was confirmed by references to Anglo-American participation studies, not for instance by previous Finnish studies (Allardt 1956; Allardt and Bruun 1956). A reference to the USA thus authorises this proposition by replacing an argument with the sign of an argument (Luostarinen and Väliverronen 1991: 96). (For critiques of the original Anglo-American participation studies, see for example Siltanen and Stanworth 1984.)

Besides being generalised over space, the 'finding' of women's passivity also seems to have been generalised over time. That a difference was found 'over a half-century ago' does not diminish the value of the generalisation; on the contrary, it begins to make the difference eternal: 'When studying children of even six years, E. Barnes, W.G. Chambers and H.H. Goddard stated over half a century ago that boys rather idealise and choose their heroes among public persons and historical figures' (Pesonen 1960b: 538).

Gender difference in political behaviour was 'found' so generally valid that it is not an exaggeration to say that it became the most general, the most law-like truth in the behavioural laws and regularities of politics, and it was these very laws and regularities that behaviourists themselves set out to discover. As the aim of the new political science was 'to find invariances, to uncover the regularities which are prevailing in the political activity and in the political attitudes of human individuals and human groups' (Teljo 1950, cited in Pesonen 1962), women seemed to form and thus to provide this kind of human (animal?) group, one that behaved in a regular and regulated manner.

Constructing political activity

So far my discussion has only dealt with how the texts frame the question of gender difference, i.e. the opening sections of the texts. Now I will put the following questions to the texts. What is political activity? How is it constructed discursively?

Because childhood socialisation 'explains' later political behaviour, studying children is important. To illustrate that point, I continue with the previous citation:

> boys idealise and choose their heroes among public persons and historical figures. Girls, instead, choose their ideals rather among their parents, teachers or friends. Schoolboys read historical novels and newspaper articles that deal with society, whereas girls are more willing to read other novels. These kinds of differences appearing at early ages should be attended to, because even as adults, men have turned out to be more 'political' than women.
>
> (Pesonen 1960b: 538)

The quotation marks around 'political' are in the original text. They seem to be highly significant: why it is that reading historical novels rather than other novels predestines children to political activity is not revealed. What makes one practice more political than another one? Gender?

'Interest in politics' is associated with the most imaginative practices. The gendered practices of the time were written into the measures of political activity, namely who reads newspapers, who listens to the radio and to what programmes, who goes to church, who discusses politics with whom – at home or at the workplace, and who talks and who merely listens. Going to public libraries to read newspapers was found to be a gendered practice that was 'explained' by the 'general' observation that men were more interested in politics than women (Rahkonen 1961).

In Pesonen (1958a), one of the main studies of student voters' behaviour in the presidential elections of 1956, there is a two-step interview, a panel study based on interview data. Students were asked about 'political activity' before the elections and afterwards. Interestingly, the acknowledged aim of the study was 'not just to study language' (ibid.: 23). Apparently the 'not just language' aim led to using structured interviews for gathering data. How this became 'something other than language' remained unexplained.

Measures of political activity were picked up from Anglo-American voting studies, already presented at the outset as hypotheses based on 'observations of the Anglo-Saxon voter', in which men were already found to be more interested in politics, discussing politics more, gathering more information about the elections, and voting more often than women (ibid.: 27). So, measures for political activity became, for example, interest in politics (ibid.: 72–4), the number of opinions (ibid.: 86–9), choosing a party (ibid.: 95). Students' activism in gathering information about the elections was measured by newspaper-reading and listening to the radio (the programmes were listed). So, let us look at the results.

Constructing results: the wonders of data analysis

Following the Pesonen study of 1958, I examine results as they are reported in the text. The narrative structure advances as follows: the chapter on 'interest in politics' starts with a normative claim that students as 'the hope of the nation' should be interested in politics. Then a reference is made to the USA and Britain, where 'politics is found to interest men more than women'. After this, the results of the survey are presented in a table and in the text, and a gender difference is confirmed. Then a conclusion is presented in bold in a separate sentence, whatever the distribution of results: 'male stu-

dents were more interested in political matters than female students'
(Pesonen 1958a: 72–4).

Looking at the text, we learn that information about 'interest in
politics' was gathered by asking the respondents: 'How interested
would you say you are in politics and governmental matters?' Who
is talking? When did the respondents' own 'verbal responses' turn
into objective reality – a fact taken at face value? The study starts to
tautologise cultural conceptions of what is considered politics, and
what is not; what is considered culturally proper gender behaviour,
and what is not. The same structure is repeated with respect to
other variables for political activity.

Soon the variables also begin to form weird quantifications and
'second-order tautologies', as in the case of 'number of opinions':
'the ones more interested in politics had more political opinions
than the ones less interested'.

The Pesonen study of 1965 also shows that analysing political
activity can be trickier than one would expect. In the comparable
1965 statistics for voting in Tampere and Korpilahti a law of positive correlations was found between different variables. The 'good
things' were cumulative: 'for those who were active, different ways
to take an interest in politics were cumulative in Korpilahti, as well
as in Tampere' (Pesonen 1965: 77). This was verified, for example,
by following results:

> The more the inhabitants of Tampere thought themselves to be
> interested in politics in May, the more actively they discussed
> politics even in July.
>
> (ibid.: 54)

In some studies it has been discovered that the number of opinions grows with growing interest. Table 3.8 shows that the previous conclusion also holds for Tampere in May 1956. The more
interested the people were, the more opinions they had. . . . On
the other hand it must be stated that party members did not have
significantly more opinions than the other inhabitants of
Tampere. Although men who belonged to parties had more opinions than other men, no such correlation was found among
women. Rather it seems that women remaining outside parties
had more political opinions than the ones belonging to parties.
No special experience seems to lie behind the volume of opinions.

> (ibid.: 71)

A correlation was found between political interest/edness – that
was different between men and women – and the value attached
to elections.

(ibid.: 74)

The information value of the correlations is especially clear in this
passage: 'Only a minority of about two fifths of the people that had
been unemployed were satisfied with their income' (ibid.: 88).

These citations illustrate 'the law of positive correlations' which
coincides with gender difference: men are more interested in politics
on any measure of interest (ibid.: 63), whereas the list of passive citizens is headed by women (ibid.: 65). The conclusions drawn from
all this are as follows:

Researchers have drawn conclusions concerning political activity,
especially on grounds of who goes to vote on polling day. Their
knowledge then actually concerns only one form of taking an
interest in politics. It may, however, be possible to define different
forms of political activity that we have not yet been able to separate clearly from each other.

(ibid.: 79)

That separating different forms of political activity may not have
been very successful in the study – that maybe the same question
was asked in different forms and correlated with itself – does not
seem to disturb the author, even though it may have occurred to the
objects of the interview: 'Even the interviewees themselves seem to
connect voting with a general interest in politics' (ibid.: 55).

Relating voting and activity

On the whole, women do not manage very well in meeting the criteria for political activity as set by the text. However, according to the
1958 study they were found to vote as actively as men. How can this
be explained? The text starts on two tracks. First, it introduces, as
an explanation, the idea that even people not interested in politics
do go out to vote, and moreover that voting is actually a less important and less reliable measure of political activity than the criteria
constructed by the political scientist himself:

Still, let us point out that mere information about participation
in elections seems to measure the political activity of the voter
groups very inexactly. Great differences occur among people
who go out to vote, and many people can in their other behav-

iour turn out to be politically passive. As stated above, even people who are not otherwise interested in politics, go out to vote.

(ibid.: 140, 147)

Second, it manages to construct a new gender difference even in voting. As Finland had two election days, the eager voters, the good guys, voted during the first day: 'Women voted, perhaps against expectations, as actively as men' (ibid.: 136).

However, of women 36% voted during the second election day, of men only 26%. If we now utilise the observation just made, according to which political activity can be observed, not just with respect to voting, but also with respect to the election day on which a person goes to vote, then male students can after all be said to be more active then female students even as voters.

(ibid.: 144)

Even in the study dating from 1965 the question of two voting days becomes centrally gendered. Husbands are seen to drag their wives to voting places, and even so, time does not seem to be the same for women, since it is said that because of the start of the summer holiday, they remain non-voters (ibid.: 256–7, 261–3, 269, 275, 280). That there might be some gendered practices, for instance in the time budgets of men and women, did not come to mind.

So, in the end, the preconception of women's passivity, in Finland and among students, was maintained. Moreover data produced by political scientists was also confirmed as more reliable than mere voting statistics.

Conclusions and results: a closure?

The final conclusions of Pesonen's 1958 study were as follows:

Men were more interested in politics than women, and were also more exposed to election propaganda. In the whole country, the percentage of men voting was higher than that for women, but students took an equally active part in elections, although a larger portion of men voted on the first election day. An equally large portion of male and female students recalled having had discussions about politics; a larger portion of women reported that they had had most of their information about elections via discussions, but men still had more opinions about politics, and –

on the basis of their manner of conversation – a larger portion
of men were considered to be political opinion leaders.

(Pesonen 1958a: 201)

Why 'manner of conversation' has suddenly become the basis of
evaluation is certainly surprising.

In the end, the conclusions drawn about Finnish students are
explained such that they follow the model of the Anglo-Saxon voter
and such that this model is valid for the whole Finnish electorate.
The conclusion is: 'the information received about Anglo-Saxon
voters with the help of panel studies, applied to our conditions, can
be assumed to hold true for Finnish voters also' (Pesonen 1958a:
201).

In spite of this 'finding', even the studies themselves would seem
to suggest a lot of evidence for another conclusion. They show that
women were not especially passive, only that their profile of behaviour differed from men's behaviour (ibid.: 29–31). It seems that
women supported parties actively and had clear opinions about
them, although they did not participate actively in them (ibid.:
36–7, 45, 189–92). Actually it seems quite easy to come to other
conclusions.

The narrative structure of research is seen as a dialogue of many
voices: (a) a voice from earlier research with which the researcher
constructs a dialogue in order to produce something new
(Luostarinen and Väliverronen 1991: 100), and (b) another voice of
reference, the voice of 'reality'. What is going on here? Instead of
producing something new, the researcher brings his own voice to the
great chorus of the Anglo-American narrative: 'women are passive
in politics'.

An afterthought: did Pesonen revise his opinions about the gen-
eralisability of the results? In an article of 1960 he was still looking
for 'internationally valid dimensions of a higher order', but this
time 'only sex and to some extent size of community correlated positively with voting turnout. Most of the results . . . contradicted
earlier findings' (Pesonen 1960a: 6). And now even female turnout
was equal to that of men, though not in the whole of Finland. This
time there is an 'explanation': 'The observed differences may be due
to different conditions in Finland and to the special character of the
population of this study. For a further comparison, the psychologi-
cal implications of social characteristics would need to be studied'
(Pesonen 1960a: 6).

Why should there be an even more private search for further

explanations? Why not notice the systematic and social character of gendered behaviour and then start studying it?

MAPPING THE CITIZENS

Ideal voters and modern orderings

What model is constructed on the basis of participation studies? What is the map? How are the voters classified?

> If only one type of division within the electorate is emphasised then no doubt facts will be simplified too much. One division is the sleepers' party, which has turned its back on society, and the other is the party of conscious citizens, who have fulfilled their obligation to vote. There are, of course, great differences among nearly two million voters. In the political system they vary from the most central and responsible to those who are most remote. Even these, however, can be influential as opinion leaders among their own acquaintances. On the other hand, many of them just content themselves with simply listening and passively following.
>
> (Pesonen 1960b: 537)

The central coordinates of the map seem to be centre-periphery, and so voter positions can be high or low (Pesonen 1962: 219). There appears to be a hierarchy in citizenship. Why does Pesonen focus on 'increasing interest in elections and political behaviour' (1962: 217)? If the map is seen in connection with a project of enhancing citizenship, it is then connected with a wider time perspective. This is actually done by Pesonen (1964) in a newspaper article. The article refers to choices made in the 1906 legislation on general suffrage in Finland. References are made to the Hermansson committee preparing the reform:

> Unfortunately, no coherent presentation was made in 1906 that would show how and on what grounds Finns were requested to make their choices among parties. We can, however, draw conclusions from some noteworthy comments on what was expected of an 'ideal voter' when general suffrage was legislated here.
>
> (Pesonen 1964: 4)

Why the 'model voter' and his/her qualities should be discussed, rather than 'the model government' and the voters' chances of controlling public power, is not specified. The qualities attached to 'the model voter' clearly have something to do with maturity, adulthood and enlightenment. The two groups that might not fulfil these criteria are the following:

1 *Youth.* Maturity seems to be required, dependence may easily lead youth astray under the sway of constitutional provocateurs who can turn the sensitive mind of youth with their mellifluous, ornate speeches and phrases to follow party aims.
2 *Women.* Another dispute dealt with women's right to vote, on which two views existed in the committee. According to some, young women, who make up a rather large part of the electorate, have on the whole so far paid very little attention to governmental and legislative matters, of which they have hardly any comprehension. And one may doubt, with reason, whether it would be good to try to bring them artificially to rapid maturity by using election laws. The majority of the committee considered, however, that married women, who are the majority, have learned in the school of life to balance reason against counter-argument.

This constructs a 'B-population' out of youth and women, whose 'independence' and 'growth into truly active politics', whose 'mature and independent discretion' and maturity are all found wanting. The maturation of these groups does not seem to have advanced much since the beginning of the century, when the vote was 'given' to these groups. The 'problem' still seems 'surprisingly fresh' to the author (Pesonen 1964: 5). The Hermansson Committee is said to have wanted particularly to 'protect young women from "rapid maturation"' (Pesonen 1960a: 6–7).

Examples of this 'B-population' are brought into the text by giving them a voice. How is this done? How is 'the other voice' treated?

In Korpilahti, an interview was conducted with one farmer's wife, who told us that she had not taken part in a single election. She had visited a voting place only once. This was in 1939, when she still was too young to vote. Two decades later she still said, offended: 'As they didn't let me go then, I haven't tried later on, either.'

Who is the stupid one here? The farmer's wife or the young student (from Helsinki?) who conducted the interview. How does the text produce the farmer's wife as ridiculous? And how can this representation be put into question? Knowing the population of the district Häme we could just as well assume that the farmer's wife was not completely literal in her speech or open about her motives.

A young woman had moved into the city and married a communist from Tampere. In May 1958 she still supported the agrarian party, which was her father's party. But in the interview conducted in July she explained that she had given her vote to the workers' union. In reality, her new opinion did not mature quite so easily; according to the notes in the election register she did not vote at all.

Even here the author puts himself on the same side as the audience, saying, see how laughable this poor voter is (Gusfield 1976). If the poor woman really did change her mind like that there would have been good reason for Finnish political scientists to study patriarchal power relations in the countryside.

How do voters fulfil the requirements of 'the ideal voter'? We can see clearly that the farmer's wife from Korpilahti (the non-voter) or the communist's wife from Tampere (the changeable voter) did not fulfil the requirements of the ideal. But the question is whether the third example (the stable voter) does that:

For instance, a retired factory worker from Tampere told us about having been a member of the social democrats from the beginning, so this in a way implies that his party affiliation of the year 1958 was decided upon up to half a decade ago.

(Pesonen 1964: 6)

'Bad' voters, for some reason, are exemplified by women, and are explicitly mentioned as women (see also Pesonen 1965: 55, 81; and according to Pesonen 1965, even the stable voter, the factory worker, was a woman). The motives, however, are attributed by the author, who does not seem to be interested in the subjects' own views of their motivations. The authority of the author to legislate on motives appears unquestionable.

The opposite of these poor souls is the interested person, discussing the elections with his friends and 'presenting the largest number of opinions' (Pesonen 1960b: 537). The conclusions of Pesonen (1965) are also clear and unambiguous: 'Above average in interest were men, especially married ones, and middle-aged and wealthy, high-earning people' (1965: 80). Discussing these 'ideal voters', the author underlines the effect of the original citation from the Hermansson Committee by marvelling yet again at how 'fresh and timely the text is' – references to a text from 1906. The article in which the references are made, however, was written in 1964. So the construction of the 'B-population' endures through time. This happens despite results based on voting statistics from 1956, and results from the author's own study of 1958, which showed that female students voted slightly more actively than male ones.

What is 'the problem' here? The texts establish differences that create the 'norm' and the 'problematic', the 'deviant' populations of voters. The 'norm' is the population not specified: not young, not female, not working class. The 'norms' themselves decide the criteria for normality, in relation to which everybody else is constructed as deviant. However 'near the voter' the researcher aims, the jurisdiction, the criteria are set by the researcher himself, as an image of himself. The right to give meaning to voting remains his. The project of citizenship has been expanded, youth and women have been integrated into citizenship, but as a 'B-population', as marginal.

Participation studies as citizen control

The vocabulary of participation studies seems to imply that voting and voting studies have something to do with constructing 'A-' and 'B-populations', and at the same time integrating and controlling citizens through a concept of 'citizenship'. The objects studied seem to be determined: 'In some countries, race, religion, nationality or "native origin" has this kind of remote-controlling effect' (Pesonen 1960b: 539). What is this knowledge for? How 'near the voter' can the enquiries extend? Looking at some of the texts, the vision becomes downright frightening: 'Even without conducting an interview, it is possible to know whether or not a particular Finnish citizen voted, simply because the election board makes notes of this in the register of voters.'

Sex, age, marital status, address, occupation and even native language are additional variables readily available from the register:

> It is possible to add data from other official and private records to this basic information such as, for instance, taxable income, length of the residence in the commune, membership in some associations, etc., for each person; and with some additional trouble, the records of previous elections can be searched, as far as they are preserved, so constant and occasional non-voters could be traced. Moreover, as this application of the law on making documents public is not widely known at all, it provides the interviewer with a reliable way of checking whether the interviewees have given correct answers regarding their participation.
>
> (Pesonen 1962: 221–2)

Since political beliefs are said to be extremely private, a second control is now introduced: official documents are used to counter-check the survey data. In this way the 'communist's wife' referred to above was revealed to be a non-voter instead of a changeable voter. The perspective for studying voting behaviour is that of surveillance (Pesonen 1958b: 369).

FACTS, OTHERS, SELVES

> The research on political behaviour is like a house. . . . Part of the foundations lie on sand, and some of the walls hang weirdly, but from the top, a marvellous view opens up.
>
> (Pesonen 1961: 207)

> Some people even take the view that research on political behaviour does not, in fact, mean anything.
>
> (Pesonen 1961: 206)

How was the 'fact' of women's passivity produced? How did it gain credibility? In the above discussion, I have been trying to establish that the 'fact' of women's' passivity is not 'true', because there is no reason to believe in it. However, I have not claimed that another fact should be produced to replace it. I have been looking at how the fact was produced rhetorically, and I expect that other facts are being produced in a similar way.

The rhetorical devices used in the texts are the ones commonly used in science in general and behavioural science in particular. The language of science appears to us to be transparent, objective, static and logical. 'Scientific-looking' language employs the usual rhetorical devices based on an 'ideology of representation' (Woolgar 1988); it makes us believe that the objects of research exist 'out there', independently of the researcher, before he starts 'looking at them' and 'finding the facts'.

The language game of the researcher produces the object of research and constructs specific kinds of identities. 'The voter' becomes a reified subject who produces reified social relations. In political science, a human being is accorded value only as this kind of reified subject. Identity is reduced to a social category (Potter and Wetherell 1987). Political activity is reduced to voting, which is also remote-controlled. The voter-identity category constructs people as controllable and countable (Rose 1990).

Among these 'voters', women are constructed as peripheral, marginal and deviant. The appalling feature of the discourse is that there is no attempt to explain women's behaviour. Gender explains it all; nothing explains gender. It is merely produced, i.e. reproduced from cultural stereotypes, classified as binary, produced as a natural category, hierarchised and eternalised.

It seems that the fact of women's passivity was imported rather than researched. The 'American' voices in the text overrode the local voices of Finnish 'reality'. Gendered practices were embedded in the way that central concepts were constructed. Analyses of data were turned into tautologisations of cultural conceptions, and into second-order tautologies – explaining nothing.

In the beginning behaviourist discourse was legitimated by referencing the real, 'getting near the voter', telling us the facts about a true reality. However 'near the voter' the researcher aims, some features of the texts reveal a contrary tendency – an aim of distancing the voter from the researcher. The language of behaviourism created conceptual totems that were translations of everyday language, for example, 'attitudes', 'behaviour', 'verbal responses' and 'verbal reactions'. What part of, for instance, my everyday life would be considered 'political behaviour'? The 'behaviour' of walking to Kallio secondary school to vote? The 'behaviour' of walking to Elanto market at Vaasanaukio to buy food? I get the feeling that the former should be considered 'political behaviour', and the latter not. But why?

The discourse was authorised by the use of metaphors from the natural sciences. Quantification and seeming exactness made the arguments all the more convincing. Methods appeared as 'tools'. It was forgotten that the questions were posed by the researcher, and his judgements were loaded with values (Shapiro 1986). Concepts and methods became totems, signs of belonging to an academic tribe, to the scientific community. They acquired magical powers (Luostarinen and Väliverronen 1991). It was essential that behaviourist texts were understood as factual discourse, not as fiction. Extra help was obtained by positioning 'Anglo-America' as a contextual ideal for the scientific community in Finnish political science at the time.

The texts produce not only 'others', but also 'selves'. Looking at the total organisation of the discourse, we can work out that the effects and consequences of it are twofold. For the researcher himself, the effects seem quite positive. Discourse followed the logic of professionalisation and established the researcher as an expert on something. It established a monopoly on giving meaning to other people's choices. If we look at the total organisation of the discourse, we see that it constructed women as deviant and limited the political to what men do. This representation may have had some effects upon women, who, of course, still voted and 'behaved', although their 'behaviour' was not culturally confirmed or acknowledged. The main effect, most probably, was on Finnish political science, which in this way established and strengthened its own professional borders.

How could anybody believe in this representation, in 'the facts'? What made it credible? Credibility is not based on rhetorical tricks alone. Neither is it based only on the social position of science as a canonical practice, which the rhetoric of behaviourism helped to heighten. That the texts were believed (I assume) is also based on 'pre-conditions and pre-contracts of argumentation', which, according to Summa (1990), are implicit. How things become facts or lose their facticity, and how things are valued or lose their value, is based on an author–audience pre-contract: a shared view of values and of hierarchical grounds for evaluation. Within the value frames of the 1950s it might not have been possible to contest the representation of women's passivity.

That I can now (I hope) produce a credible counter-text and illustrate the non-logic of behaviourist texts is not because former political scientists were stupid whereas we are now so clever. Destabilising and questioning the author–audience reading contract is now possible because of contextual changes. Facticity is now put into question because of the passage of time and because of the change in social conventions and values. The 'value kit' of the practitioners of behaviourist 'logic' has vanished.

So what? What exactly has changed? There are some signs that seem to indicate that gender as a natural category was seen as problematic very soon after the Pesonen texts were published. The author himself in a book of 1972 refers to another study of 1966, and states that the respondents of an interview might gear their answers in accordance with the cultural expectations and norms relating to gendered behaviour (Pesonen 1972: 71). Also, Jansson, in 1966, wrote that the 'fact' of women's passivity should also be explained and culturally contextualised, and that change in this respect was possible and even desirable.

One problem still arises here. We now know that people may say what they are expected to say, i.e. speak as their culture 'conditions' them to speak. Does that also mean that the political scientist perhaps asks what he is expected to ask – what his cultural context, his gender, age or any other 'background variable' conditions him to ask? Is this going on even now?

7 Dimensions of the political
Travel and interpretation

Kari Palonen

Hans Magnus Enzensberger's *Ach Europa!* (1987) is difficult to classify by literary genre. It is neither an essay on Europe as a cultural concept, like Edgar Morin's *Penser l'Europe* (1987), nor a journalistic report on current events like Timothy Garton Ash's *The Uses of Adversity* (1989) and *We The People* (1990). Nor is it a handbook for political tourists, and it is least of all a textbook on 'European political systems'. In this chapter I use it to illustrate a strategy for 'reading the political' in terms of its own (Palonen 1993a).

Enzensberger (b. 1929) is a West German writer and publicist, and the former editor of *Kursbuch*, a journal that played a key role for left intellectuals in the 1960s and 1970s. In an interview before the 1987 Bundestag elections, Enzensberger appealed for a replacement of the centralistic, governmental paradigm of politics and instead proposed a consideration of politics as a self-organised array of diverse ideas and interests (1988: 230). Enzensberger adopts the nominalist view that politics is not fixed on some objects and absent from others, but is always a question of interpretation. The perspective of self-organised individuals enables him to read 'the political' in seemingly trivial phenomena.

Read in the perspective of conceptual history, Enzensberger's view of politics can be seen as an expression of the pro-political sub-current among twentieth-century German literati. The word *Politisierung* was coined by Karl Lamprecht in 1907, and it was later given different interpretations, especially by the Expressionists Kurt Hiller (1973) and Ludwig Rubiner (cf. Palonen 1989). Since then the word has been adopted into other languages, and the idea of reinterpreting some phenomenon as political, as something to which alternative and conflicting standpoints can be attached, has become almost a commonplace (Palonen 1993a). Among mainstream political scientists politicisation is still suspect. They tend to see it as a marginal phenomenon in comparison with the 'polity' or the 'political system' in their conception of politics.

Enzensberger belongs to the literati who believe that every polity is based on politicisation, not the other way round. He has no problem with detecting aspects and dimensions of 'the political' in questions outside the terms of conventional political science. It also allows him to doubt, as Kurt Hiller had done already in 1911, whether governments, parliaments, parties and politicians are acting politically at all (1988: 230). I intend to reconstruct the way that 'the political' is read in *Ach Europa!*. My special concerns are language, space and time as constitutive dimensions of 'the political', as well as a methodology of research-by-travelling.

TRAVELLING: CENTRES AND PERIPHERIES

By 1972 Enzensberger had published an essay, 'Revolutionstourismus', parodying the tendency of many left-wing intellectuals to accept a fellow-traveller role as 'delegation tourists', who were not allowed to walk about unaccompanied in the city they were visiting (quoting Susan Sontag's words after a visit to Hanoi – Enzensberger 1973: 162). 'Delegation tourists' still tended to claim the status of 'expert' after visits of only some weeks (quoting a poem by Herberto Padilla – Enzensberger 1973: 131). One notable aspect of *Ach Europa!* is the author's tacit opposition to delegation tourism.

Another essay by Enzensberger that is important for understanding *Ach Europa!* is 'Resozismus' (1982). The title is an abridgement of a self-parodying name for the Soviet sphere during the Brezhnev era. It refers to the 'highest stage of underdevelopment', especially to the fact that East European countries were not allowed to do better than the Soviet Union. When visiting Hungary and Poland in the early or mid-1980s, Enzensberger did not have the illusions held by many Western leftists concerning the inherent potential of these systems. However, it is this disillusionment that also gave him a chance to regard East European countries outside the cold war framework.

Like Morin and Garton Ash, Enzensberger comes from a political centre in Europe. He visits only peripheral countries – Sweden, Italy, Hungary, Portugal, Norway, Poland and Spain – but compares them not only with each other but also with the central countries, thus relativising the opposition between centre and periphery (1989b), saying, for instance, that students in Tromsø in Norway have in many respects better conditions for studying than their colleagues in the major centres, such as Paris or Munich (1987: 233).

Unlike Garton Ash, Enzensberger does not attempt to manifest himself wherever 'something is happening'; on the contrary he travels where 'nothing happens' (1987: 335; 1989a: 193). His references also mention things that are absent, that which is 'not Europe' – 'Bhopal, Luanda, La Paz' (1987: 162; 1989a: 120), as well as that which 'is Europe' – 'Zagreb, Brno, Budapest, Wien, Kraków, Trieste, Berlin' (1987: 344; 1989a: 200).

The plurality of eccentric viewpoints is a central dimension in Enzensberger's use of travelling as a method. But unlike quotations or interviews in the political travel literature, these curiosities do not serve to illustrate aspects of the country or current events there. They rather give the author an opportunity to distance himself further from what he observes. A Portuguese monsignore, speaking of 'time islands', gives Enzensberger the hint for the model of a time machine, allowing him to present the final chapter of the book as a report in the *New Yorker* of 26 February 2006, written (supposedly) by Timothy Taylor (1987: 182–3; 1989a: 135–6). Enzensberger's collage bears some resemblance to *Utopia* by Thomas More (1516), a classical model for a work mixing the genres of quotation and authorial commentary.

TRAVELLING IN THE HORIZON OF NAMES

A linguistic turn renders travel stories into travels between names. What is encountered and noteworthy consists of names of cities, persons, events, streets, sometimes used as symbols or metonymies for events, etc. The horizon of names in a book tracks the intellectual horizon of the author. Another characteristic in travel stories is wondering about strange names, which become independent of their reference. *Ach Europa!* cannot be understood without attending to wordplay.

Unfortunately, there is no index of names in *Ach Europa!* I have made lists of the names of persons, cities and streets. For persons and cities I have noticed only contextual references, concerning names outside the subject matter of the chapters. Street names, however, are more directly linked to subject matter and should be considered carefully. Well-known names are at the head of the list:

* Hitler: 251, 318, 330, 331, 345, 396, 399, 473
* Marx: 38, 139, 255, 305, 313, 417, 465

- Lenin: 137 ff, 157, 160, 326, 430
- Engels: 121, 417, 465
- Stalin: 372, 408, 491.

All five names have cast shadows on post-war Europe. Indeed, Lenin is the only person in *Ach Europa!* who is also mentioned in the lists of cities and streets (Lenin-Ring [Lenin-körút] in Budapest). Persons other than these five appear in the book only sporadically, e.g. Reagan as a symbol for evil in Spain, while the names Kohl, Thatcher, Mitterrand or even Brezhnev and Gorbachev are absent. The governments of today represent for Enzensberger only paper tigers (cf. 1988: 229), for whom there is no need of canonisation or demonisation. Enzensberger's name horizon is literary and academic. No sportsman/woman and only one pop star (Nina Hagen, 158) is mentioned.

The head of the list for city names is as follows:

- Paris: 109, 153, 200, 215, 283, 293, 302, 320, 333, 393, 425, 462, 489
- Moscow: 122, 144, 170, 197, 252, 366, 383, 407
- New York: 89, 178, 183, 290, 383, 459, 489, 497
- Berlin: 9, 106, 325, 344, 427, 454, 492
- Frankfurt: 9, 91, 104, 106, 108, 134
- Stockholm: 81, 103, 109, 258, 277, 392 (outside the chapter on Sweden)
- Copenhagen: 104, 255, 456, 465
- London: 103, 246, 459, 462
- Brussels: 103f, 479ff
- Bonn: 33, 102, 425
- Jerusalem: 317, 344, 434
- Vienna: 326, 344, 488.

As the paradigm for a centred conception of Europe *à la* Morin, Paris appears as the leading reference, even for Enzensberger's travels in Europe's peripheries. Moscow, New York and Berlin are other centres, to which it is easy to compare cities and lives in the periphery. London appears only as a sub-centre, like Stockholm or Copenhagen. Absent from the whole story are sub-centres in countries not visited by Enzensberger, e.g. Riga, Marseille, Århus, Graz or Glasgow, while Bucharest, Prague and Helsinki are mentioned only as places visited in the final chapter by 'Taylor'.

Enzensberger's style of establishing reference by listing cities is also remarkable. Some of them are less cities than metonymies:

Yalta, Bhopal, The Klondyke. But Rugby does not refer to the game, and neither does Bad Godesberg refer to the SPD party platform of 1959. He also uses two Paris street names metonymically: Champs-Elysées (1987: 227) and Quai d'Orsay (1987: 252), the latter, of course, as a double metonymy, referring to the site of the French foreign ministry.

In *Ach Europa!* the use of street names, as opposed to city names, is less significant. In chapters on Sweden and Italy, street names only serve the purpose of localising events or rendering them familiar to other visitors. Enzensberger does not thematise 'the political' in common Western street names (cf. Azaryahu 1990; Palonen 1993b), but tends rather to regard changes of name as reflections of regime changes, like the triad Saxony Square/Adolf Hitler Square/Victory Square in Warsaw (1987: 330; 1989a: 189; cf. also changes in the names of Polish provinces, 1987: 339; 1989a: 196). The result of these changes appears to him often paradoxical: calling a business centre in Budapest Karl Marx Square is an insult to Marx (1987: 138–9; 1989a: 101). In Lódz the rhetoric of names depends more on the audience than on authoritative decisions directed at them:

> the Street of the Siege of Stalingrad, only no one calls it that. Its old patriotic name, Street of the Eleventh of November, has withstood every rebaptism
>
> (1989a: 223).

As opposed to the name changes engineered from above in Eastern Europe – many of them, like Lenin-Ring in Budapest, rebaptised again after 1989 – there is the use of anachronistic names that have lost their original reference. For example, the old 'monarchical' names in Western cities are so evident that even a visitor does not usually pay attention to them, even if they dominate the whole city text, as in Munich. Enzensberger's favourite anachronisms concern Norwegian newspapers:

> The best side of Norwegian newspapers are their touching, quaint, and bizarre titles. In Kristiansand one reads the *Friend of the Fatherland* and the *Challenge of the Times*, in Lillehammer the *Spectator*, in Tromsø the *Northern Light*, in Oslo the *Course of the World*, in Asker the *Messenger's Walking Stick* and in Horten the *Returner*.
>
> (1987: 286–7)

Attention to anachronisms of this kind is an obvious advantage that accrues to the method of travelling: to a Norwegian, *Verdens Gang* refers only to the paper, not to what's happening in the world. Taking such references at face value gives Enzensberger a further indicator of the curious rhythm of time in Norway.

Another typical case of paradoxes in the presentation and use of names comes from Budapest letterboxes. A whole set of politically relevant situations can be read from them.

> Then the names on the innumerable letter boxes: names crossed out, illegible, smeared in felt-tip, faded, machine-punched, written with a flourish in brown ink. They reveal more than any statistic: there are not enough apartments in Budapest, here every square yard must be conquered with fantastic schemes and defended with dogged skill. The proliferating nameplates speak of exchanges, of allocations, of corruption, of inheritances, dividing walls, divorces, of odysseys of flight from the land and of emigration, of illegal business deals and laborious repairs, of unconquerable desire and of this city's inventive chaos.
>
> (1989a: 103)

Running counter to anachronism there are also attempts to adapt 'to the requirements of the time' in order to improve one's own position against competitors. This is the case with the names of Swedish bourgeois parties, which are unwittingly colourless and defensive:

> The Conservatives call themselves the Moderate Union Party, as if they were ashamed of being Conservatives. The Liberals clearly find their own Liberalism suspect, so they've settled on a folksier name, while the old Farmer's Party hides behind a title so neutral that it hardly means anything at all.
>
> (1989a: 6)

However, Enzensberger's argument presupposes a priority of realities over names. Changing party names can also be judged as attempts to break with nineteenth-century 'isms' as a necessary condition for restructuring the whole political spectrum in a manner that would no longer support the Social Democratic hegemony. One hint of this hegemony is the substantialisation and subjectivisation of the concept 'society' (*samhället*) in Swedish political language. Enzensberger's remarks on this rhetorical figure in the language of political parties, bureaucrats and trade unions in Sweden give good examples of nominalistic, 'deconstructive' rhetoric:

They believe they are able to speak and act not only in the name of their own organisations but of society as a whole. Certain characteristic phrases recur in their statements: 'Society must intervene here.' 'Society cannot allow this.' 'Society must concern itself with this.' Reading the sentences more carefully, one soon realises that the word *samhället* (society) is synonymous with 'the institution I represent'.

(1989a: 15)

According to Enzensberger, the hegemony of the Swedish Social Democrats remains fragile because of the absence of the symbolic dimension. 'Society' as a symbol is too abstract in order to be effective. In this respect, Enzensberger is in line with theorists of the specificity of 'the political' – like Max Weber, Hannah Arendt, Jean-Paul Sartre and Michael Oakeshott – theorists who refuse to subordinate politics to the idea of 'society'. The language of 'the political' rejects the subordination of human actions to the depoliticising language of processes, functions, etc.

The way that names in *Ach Europa!* are thematised politically can certainly be criticised from a nominalist point of view. Even the most trivial street names appear as political, as results of decisions which could have been otherwise, and thus at any time a potential source of conflict (Palonen 1993b). Naming is a political act *par excellence* in so far as it creates new realities through definitions (Benjamin 1983: 643–54). The Budapest letterboxes can be read as an example of the presence of 'the political' in giving, using and changing names. Playing with names, both as a politicisation of a situation and as politicking within an already politicised horizon, has been explored, for example, in feminist politics (Pusch 1990).

GRAFFITI AS A LANGUAGE OF THE POLITICAL SPACE

Naming is perhaps the most obvious aspect of the linguistic dimension of the political, but there are others that immediately attract the traveller's attention. The plurality of natural languages and the struggles between them are an inalienable part of Enzensberger's concept of Europe: 'Taylor' wonders, for instance, why the notes of the European Community are printed in twelve languages (1987: 455; 1989a: 287). Enzensberger himself admires the Norwegian practice of using two languages, even when they are close to each other: the result of the language struggle is that everything must be expressed in two languages, including 'the translation of the Odyssey and the telex formula' (1987: 248).

Enzensberger understands the tendency to create new languages for each region in post-Franco Spain. His doubts begin when he finds that this can lead to 'linguistic civil wars', to a 'tower of Babel' in Spanish territory. For the individual the plurality of available languages tends to vanish again when regional linguistic monopolies appear:

> It is also entirely reasonable for the inhabitants of Barcelona to demand that the city have street signs not only in Spanish but in the language of the country, too. Yet hardly has this goal been attained than the local language guerillas set to work obliterating every single Spanish word.

> (1989a: 275)

Spray-painting also gets close attention in *Ach Europa!* Graffiti as expression and means of politicking is a further aspect of the linguistic dimension of politics that Enzensberger discusses, especially in the Iberian peninsula. In the Basque country, graffiti are simple expressions of a separatist politics of protest, without any aestheticisation of politics:

> Here, unlike in Madrid, painting graffiti is no sport for outsiders: it is not an outlet for sectarians, not an alibi for students from the lower middle class, but a collective obsession. The writing on the wall only expresses what everyone thinks, and, whatever the signature, the words – which I can understand, though I don't speak a word of Basque – always say the same thing. 'Clear out forever! Out!' The addressee, the Spanish state and its representatives, is nowhere to be seen.

> (1989a: 267)

As opposed to an instrumental view of 'politics by graffiti', the Portuguese revolution for Enzensberger expresses something quite different. To Enzensberger's retrospective judgement the revolution appeared as an opportunity to express oneself politically by means of graffiti:

> And best of all, the walls of the city were covered with coloured signs and pictures overnight. Everyone painted and wrote what he wanted – painted dreams sprang up, utopias ran wild across the façades as far as hands could reach. It was political intoxication, bright, tropical, psychedelic, uninhibited. Not a monologue

but a babble of voices, a delirious abundance of desires: and for everyone, justice for all, the test pattern of a better world projected onto the crumbling plasterwork of an old city.

(1989a: 149)

The revolution was an extraordinary situation, giving an opportunity for everyone to express publicly their own opinions. The public space was re-created and coloured by the simple means of graffiti. For the interpreter, the graffiti, still more or less present years after the end of the revolution, give the only hints left about the plurality and individuality of the views expressed in the revolutionary situation, but hardly noticed by the conventional struggle of parties and groupings later in the revolutionary era. Enzensberger also comments on the ambiguous end of this euphoria:

> I don't know if gangs of cleaners turned up one day with pails and brushes to remove this total art work, but I doubt it. No such thorough, systematic administration exists in Portugal. I believe the sea of pictures disappeared of its own accord. Indifference, rain, disappointment effaced the writing, washed away the traces.

(1989a: 149)

For Enzensberger the remnants of the revolutionary graffiti are ambivalent. They refer to the fact that no repression was actually needed to end the revolution, rather fatigue was enough. Simultaneously they refer to the reality of creative expression, which, as faded fragments, still gives an opportunity to rethink the political chances represented in the Portuguese revolution. Politicisation cannot be ended intentionally, and depoliticisation consists in its exhaustion and disappearance.

For readers of Enzensberger, the politicisation of space by means of graffiti implicitly refers to the biggest *Gesamtkunstwerk* in the world, to the western side of the Berlin Wall. The transformation of the Wall into a monumental 'mural journal' is a manifest expression of the contingency of history, something that no politician either in the East or in the West could have imagined in 1961. The fate of the Wall after 1989 – its fall was 'predicted' by Enzensberger in 1987 – is a sign of the dominance of old-style politicians over individual agents politicking and politicising by means of graffiti. Why was the opportunity for this kind of politics not granted on the eastern side of the Wall?

'Timothy Taylor' visits Berlin in 2006, after the fall of the Wall.

In Enzensberger's imagination nobody wanted to destroy the Wall. But an intensive struggle was going on between the partisans of a 'biotope' and of the *Gesamtkunstwerk*. 'Taylor's' tourist guide from the 'biotope' party describes the situation thus:

> The art historians are the worst. They regard the Wall as a work of art because of the graffiti, which are, however, only to be found on the western side. The Senator responsible for the arts would like to make a twenty-mile long open-air museum out of the 'biotope'.
>
> (1989a: 299)

The linguistic dimension of politics has in general been understood better by writers and literati than by professional political scientists or philosophers. But the quasi-Machiavellian approach, also advocated by Enzensberger in his 'realist' moods, separates words and deeds, language and reality from each other. This hardly appears plausible today. Now we understand better than ever the thesis from the philosopher J.L. Austin (1990) that words are deeds. Every use of words has potentially political aspects, and graffiti as a means of expression deserve the attention of political scientists, too.

THE PRESENCE OF THE PAST IN POLITICAL SPACE

Spatial metaphors have dominated established politics, and in a metonymic manner politics is often linked with activities taking place in definite spaces, in parliaments, electoral meetings, etc. The ritualisation of conventional politics has sometimes resulted in curious depoliticisations of paradigmatic political spaces. In *Ach Europa!* this is exemplified by the priority of tourism over legislation in the Hungarian Parliament House:

> There is no sign of work here. There aren't any offices for the MPs. . . . But the representatives of the people meet only four weeks a year, for two whole days at a time. For fifty-one weeks out of fifty-two the chamber serves the tourist trade.
>
> (1989a: 108)

Today we might also ask again whether the 'democratic' parliament in Hungary is mainly a tourist attraction. Elsewhere spaces have been politicised by historical events, like the small Spanish town Marinaleda. After repeated land occupations, it has become a 'rhetorical village' for the left (1987: 419; 1989a: 259).

Both the ancient polis and medieval autonomous cities had an inherent political dimension, and politics was understood as something specific to European cities (Weber 1980). For Enzensberger graffiti in contemporary cities appear as one form of politicking, rendering politics visible for the many, as opposed to the closed world of cabinet-style politics. It is no wonder that attitude towards graffiti has become a subtle watershed in European municipal politics.

The opposition between 'political' cities in Europe and depoliticised 'car-cities' in America is another spatial aspect of politics, emphasised by Enzensberger in his judgements. This is one of the main reasons for his preference for Oslo over Stockholm:

> The Oslo I like is time-warped, dirty, untidy, chaotic; a town that knows how to take care of itself. Here, modern city planning has suffered one humiliation after another. The vandalism of the planners that succeeded in erasing Stockholm's city centre failed miserably here because of Oslo's dynamic sloth, its stubborn mix-ups. Here, the technocratic obsession with the 'car-friendly' city never stood a chance.
>
> (1987: 258)

Here space is connected with the presence of history, a reference to past times. Enzensberger's other favourite among European cities is Lisbon, where pre-modern contingency in the division of space as against 'social apartheid' among modern buildings is still visible (1987: 187; 1989a: 139–40). The division into rich and poor, however, is not a sufficient reason to depoliticise the city. In the old Warsaw suburb of Praga, history is present as a reminder of 'pre-war time with its older vitality and misery' (1987: 323; 1989a: 183).

Ach Europa!, of course, is overshadowed by global divisions of the world in the post-war era. The reference to Yalta cannot be overestimated. The thesis from the *Resozismus* essay is used in his chapters on Hungary and Poland in order to make manifest the traces of the Third World within Europe. Enzensberger quotes the well-known Polish journalist Ryszard Kapuscinski:

> I come from a remote little hole in White Russia. I always feel ill at ease in Paris or London. I am the Third World. My work depends on it. I understand what's happening in San Salvador, in Iran, or Ethiopia, because I'm a Pole.
>
> (1989a: 209)

Before 1989 Eastern Europe, as Enzensberger sees it, was not a homogeneous political space – the division into First and Third

World went right through it. This was partly due to historical links to Western political culture, as the contrast between the cities Katowice and Kraców makes clear: 'Katowice (Kattowitz) is a Prussian industrial hell – Duisburg is idyllic by comparison; Kraków, humiliatingly neglected but still glorious, is, by contrast, an ancient Central European city: Polish Renaissance, Austrian Baroque, Viennese nineteenth-century' (1989a: 215).

The relativity of centres to peripheries is one of the main topics of *Ach Europa!*. The example of Tromsø University makes reference to the fact that in the present world distances need not be absolute obstacles any more, and, in some cases, a peripheral position even offers advantages for modernisation in practical matters. The former president of the European Community, Erkki Rintala, can retire (fictionally) in 2006 to 'Rääkkylänmäki' in the Finnish periphery without a hamburger bar (1987: 477; 1989a: 304). He does not retire from politics but gains an opportunity to rethink matters. The direction of modernisation appears as an open question – the possibility to reject fashion is an obvious advantage in the periphery. Again, it is Norway that gives the paradigm:

> Living in Norway never required one to be chic and à jour as is the case with the poor Parisians. . . . Very successfully, the country managed to distance itself from the silly customs and conventions of the middle class whose cultural hegemony in all other industrialized countries is a matter of fact. It did so even though the predominant part of the Norwegian population works in the so-called tertiary sector and, accordingly, should be regarded as petit bourgois.
>
> (1987: 302)

Political space cannot be measured – it is mediated through experiences. This idea is expressed most clearly with respect to another favourite country of Enzensberger's, Portugal. The relativity of both space and time is the thesis of a Portuguese monsignore, who views his country as an island, like Ireland, a remnant of the mythical continent Atlantis:

> Everything that Portugal needs, from peanuts to the brand-new chemical plant, is imported by ship or plane, as is to be expected on an island. . . . The continent is far away, as far away as Brazil or India. . . . Emigration is an old curse of the country, and for most people Europe is a place of exile.
>
> (1989a: 134)

The experience of discontinuity at the border between Spain and Portugal appears more important than the continuity on the map. This figure is radicalised in the final passage of the 'Taylor' story when Enzensberger inserts a reference to a poem by Ingeborg Bachmann, *Böhmen am Meer*, into the experience of a Prague taxi driver:

> —— I study in the taxi while I'm waiting. I'm an Austrian but I've been living in Prague for ten years. I'm prone to asthma and the sea air suits me.
> —— The sea air?
> —— Yes, don't you remember? The seacoast of Bohemia.
>
> (1989a: 321)

The political significance of the relativity of space is also manifested in a preference for plurality over similarity, for difference over unity. Using Erkki Rintala as his spokesman, Enzensberger finds the European unity a chimera: 'The idea originated at a time when the whole world still believed in technological progress, growth and rationalization' (1989a: 307).

Rintala rises up against power monopolies, unity by force, homogenisation, and stands up for diversity and difference. He strives for 'European unity without unity' (1987: 482; 1989a: 308). Expressed in the language of politics, this becomes: Europe does not form a single polity but a specific space for politicking with different forms of power sharing in the Weberian sense (Weber 1994: 36).

TRAVELLING AS A TIME MACHINE

In *Vergangene Zukunft* Reinhart Koselleck (1979) uses a spatial analogy and divides time into a horizon of expectations and a space of experiences. This dualism is also inherent in the time experience of the traveller: horizon of expectation is directed towards something new and subjective, but is mediated through the space of experiences. According to Koselleck, the gap between past experiences and expectations about the future has grown since the Enlightenment, so the traveller's politics of time is different.

Enzensberger opposes the utopian pictures of the future dreamed up by planners and ideologists and speaks instead about how the future demonstrates the failure of all plans (cf. the Budapest letterboxes). Even the description of 'past futures', like the graffiti of the Portuguese revolution, is distancing in tone. The only horizon of expectation present in the book is the fictive one. In Lódz Enzensberger provokes a debate about the results of 'free elections' if they were to be held next day (1987: 376; 1989a: 227). The 'Taylor' essay can be read as a fiction about the future past.

Of course, for a traveller the history of cities visited is of special interest. One important reason for Enzensberger's striking preference for Norway over Sweden, and for Portugal over Spain, lies in differing attitudes towards the past. Besides destroying the character of their cities, a capital failure of the Swedish Social Democrats lies in neglecting the history of their own country. Enzensberger wonders whether it is better for Swedish schoolchildren to 'know more about repression and exploitation in the Third World than they do about Sweden's own period as a great power' (1987: 39; 1989a: 27). The Social Democratic pathos of the future and the omnipresence of *samhället* is transmitted to the schools through the replacement of history by 'social studies'.

> L., a seventeen-year-old from Västerås, is passionately interested in the history of her country. She wants to be an historian. Two years before her graduation from school, one of her teachers explains to her that she is on the wrong track altogether. 'What's the point of all this worn-out rubbish? Do you think it means anything? You'd be much better off worrying about the future. History isn't a proper subject at all. Look at our curriculum. Social studies and more social studies, that's what we have to concentrate on.'
>
> (1989a: 25–6)

Enzensberger quotes a Norwegian historian, who considers it fatal to forget the past ahead of the coming crisis (1987: 39; 1989a: 27). That the Swedes still believe in the idea of history as a success story is perhaps not so strange. It is strange, however, that the same idea is also presented in Spain, as if the Spanish Social Democrats could simply follow the Swedes on the path of modernisation and progress. The rhetoric of progress appears as a movement without events, like the Civil War. Enzensberger quotes a writer from Gijon:

> Dynamics without change, lethargic recklessness, nothing is digested. Before a problem is solved, it's already out of date. The result is a very specific form of amnesia. Take the Civil War, for example! Of course, in reality it's anything but forgotten. But the

memory has been put in deep freeze. All the difficult problems
are shelved.

(1989a: 247)

In Poland, Hungary and even in Norway, on the contrary, nearly
everyone is an amateur historian (1987: 171, 272, 331). In Norway,
this is relatively harmless, an expression of the Norwegian way of
living a rhythm different from that of people on the continent:

Norway's clocks have always shown a different time. This country is the kingdom of temporal disjuncture, as perceptive
observers noticed early on. Ernst Sars, the famous historian,
coined a term for this failure to march in time: 'den norske
utakt'.

(1987: 310)

The Hungarians are proud of their long history, but they have
'too many skeletons in the closet' (1987: 171; 1989a: 128). In Poland
the remembrance of things past is a real obsession. Taking his
tourist guide Jadwiga as an example, Enzensberger describes this:

My head was reeling with places, names, and dates: 1768, 1941,
1830, 1981, 1794, 1863, 1944. But months and day are charged
with significance as well as the years: the 1st of August and
November 11th, the 3rd of May and December 13th . . . and
the 24th of March. A calendar shot through with red-letter days,
full of echoes, intimations, analogies. . . . most Poles have mas-
tered this patriotic cabalistic lore. They are professionals when it
comes to remembering.

(1989a: 190)

If in Norway and in Hungary history is a factor in the present, in
Poland politicking consists largely of remembrances of the past.
Even the Nazis did not find a remedy against it – they could not
'kill the dead' (1987: 333–4; 1989a: 190). The paradigm for this sort
of politicking with memory is Warsaw's Old Town, remade after
1945, despite the poverty and lack of everything – 'the largest but
also the most marvellous forgery in the world' (1987: 321–2;
1989a: 182).

Enzensberger's remarks on the way that time stops are very interesting politically. In them there is an implicit reference to Walter
Benjamin's idea of the *Jetztzeit*, 'now-time', which stops the time
from elapsing. It signifies a politicising extension of the present as
well as an actualisation of some aspect of the past by means of a

'tiger jump' (1980: theses XVI, XVII). Benjamin's 'now-time' means a 'movement in standstill'. The stopping of time in Salazar's Portugal, for instance, signified a political embalming, sheltering a past world against change from outside:

> A whole country enbalmed like a mummy for forty years! That was Salazar's achievement. Time stood still. All the deposed kings of the world found a safe heaven here, behind the walls of the regime. It was teeming with servants: pianists were flown in from all over the world for the bourgeoisie's parties. A paradise for parasites, social coma for everyone else. In his own way Salazar was a utopian, too. He wanted a world in which nothing moved, total hypnosis.
>
> (1989a: 151)

With his sensitivity to anachronism Enzensberger is not without an admiration for this project. But in Madrid's Army Museum, stopping time has led to total simultaneity, to an eternity without history (cf. Maier 1987 on the fascist concept of time as eternity):

> History has been abolished in this palace on the Calle de Méndez Núnez. Everything is synchronous – the Middle Ages and the Civil War, Pizarro and Napoleon, the Berbers and the Indios. An ossified eternity rules in this glorious panopticon. . . . War is a single, total work of art.
>
> (1989a: 242–3)

The Portuguese and Spanish ways of stopping time are parodies of Benjamin's project. Enzensberger's critique of Swedish historiography is also much in Benjamin's spirit, with his proposal to re-actualise a neglected period, 'the time of freedom', with its party strife, but also with 'intellectual fresh air and political "chaos" ' (1987: 39; 1989a: 27), which is seldom discussed today.

The title of a book *Back to the Year 1960* by some left-wing Norwegians (1987: 281) hardly signifies a 'tiger jump' in Benjamin's sense. It corresponds rather to Ernst Bloch's idea of non-simultaneity (1970), which forms the ground for Enzensberger's fascination with Norway, at the same time a museum and a laboratory for the future.

> What I find puzzling about this small, peripheral society is the unconscious feat it managed to perform time and time again over the last 170 years: it lags behind its time and yet succeeds in being ahead of it. On the one hand, it is fond of anachronisms

and tenaciously holds on to pre-modern modes of thought and ways of life. On the other hand, it leans towards an unscrupulous anticipation of the future. Such conditions do not allow for a homogeneous and even development. All this sheds some light on the dual character of the inhabitants of this country which foreign observers have noted time and again: they are both parochial and cosmopolitan at the same time. Today, Norway is Europe's largest folkloristic museum and also a vast laboratory of the future.

(1987: 310–11)

Following the quotation, this dual temporality also corresponds to a dual relation between centres and peripheries. Although archaism dominates in Portugal, it also offers a resource for resistance against technocratic modernisation:

Because what the Portuguese set against capitalist rationality is not simply incompetence but resistance. It's certainly difficult to tell one from the other. In any case, the result is a kind of silent sabotage that is not practiced out of anger, conviction, resentment, ideology, or defiance, as it is elsewhere. They don't attack capitalist efficiency, they avoid it, spontaneously, 'just like that', because it's not self-evident to the Portuguese, because the virtues it demands are not theirs.

(1989a: 176)

However old-fashioned this resistance may be, Enzensberger looks to it for a model for an alternative form of politics. It is a politics of defending stubbornly certain hopes which cannot be taken away. If they are allowed to play a role in politics, Portugal would be a great European power, envied by its neighbours (1987: 232; 1989a: 176–7).

Enzensberger's admiration for Portugal is connected with travelling in time, a central topic of the book. A Portuguese monsignore tells Enzensberger that travels into the past are free in Portugal: unlike New York, a firm called 'Second Childhood' is not needed. The Monsignore presents a 'topography of time' in terms of transcending time zones measured by 'isochrones'.

I have often asked myself what a topography of time would look like. . . . Let us assume that we are really living in 1986 – a bold assumption! – and we visited a small town in Mecklenburg. It might perhaps appear to us that the date there was 1958. A settlement in the Amazon could be dated 1935 and a monastery in Nepal assigned to the Napoleonic period. On such a map, and this is really my point, large parts of Portugal would appear as time-islands.

(1989a: 135–6)

The temporalisation of space is a central rhetorical figure in *Ach Europa!* It renders time and space commensurable with each other. Norwegian non-simultaneity is characterised, in opposition to the Portuguese version, by the presence of a long past, by the possibility of going both towards the past and towards the future.

For Enzensberger the analogies between space and time are based not only on the inspiration of the Portuguese clergyman but are rather closely linked to the experience of travelling. Travelling transcends the quasi-natural, measurable objectivities of both space and time, so reliable in 'normal' situations. For Enzensberger travelling has become a way of life, an insurance against falling back into normalcy, a move back to the circular time or 'labour' in the Arendtian sense, or to the linear time of the ideologies of progress (Arendt 1958).

For a traveller 'progress' is absurd. To relate a journey as a linear progression does not make sense. To seek the latest expressions of progress by travelling would render the comparison between experiences of the encountered world and the lived-in world impossible. If the travel report were confined to a story about which country or city at the present moment is 'in', i.e. leads the competition in progress, it would be extremely boring. If the idea of travel were to search only for progress, nobody would travel any longer.

THE ART OF TRAVELLING AS A POLITICAL CHOICE

As a final theme I will take up the activity of travelling itself, the political dimension in choice between means of travelling. Enzensberger does not say much about it – he starts always from the country visited. Still, the details in *Ach Europa!* contain valuable hints about politicking through choice between means of transport.

By using a topography of time Enzensberger thematises the means of travelling in his final chapter concerning 'Europe 2006'. A movement back and forth in both time and space appears to him as something specifically European, as opposed to American, as Americans live in the linear time of 'modernity'. 'Taylor' can hardly bear the fact that in Europe cars belong to the past and he is obliged to take the train:

Free movement in this country was impossible. Compulsory travel by train contributed to the feeling. The train to Kaiserslautern was good, even luxurious, but I would rather have gone by car, and the bureaucratic limitations on road travel exasperated me. I prepared myself for a boring journey. My fellow travellers brought out their books. That, too, was a European fad.

(1989a: 287)

The utopian aspect, the liberation of European cities from cars, is described in The Hague:

There are still a couple of taxis at the station, but they only go to the suburbs. As in most European cities, the center of town is blocked off. After a week I already have a corn on my foot.

(1989a: 289)

In Finland, the car-party still dominates: the geographical distances are so great that 'railroad mania never took hold here' (1987: 476; 1989a: 303). 'Taylor' can rent a car for his improvised visit to Erkki Rintala in Rääkkylänmäki. But although Rintala shows him a car, he also presents it as a souvenir from the era of modernity – beautiful but useless (1987: 485; 1989a: 310).

About his preferences concerning the means of transportation Enzensberger is explicit. In the chapter on Hungary he writes – against the habit of not going anywhere impossible to reach by car – 'Then we'll go on foot' (1987: 155; 1989a: 115). The pro-train position is also manifested by his use of railway hours as a time–space measuring unit (1987: 155, 488; 1989a: 115, 313). Railway stations are a key topic: their history, architecture and aesthetics are discussed in Budapest (1987: 138; 1989: 111), in a small Portuguese town called Beja – 'The lonely railway station, built in 1940, looks as if it dated from 1912' (1987: 215; 1989a: 163) – and in Lódz, where the name of the railway station is Fabryczyna (1987: 370; 1989a: 222). The political dimension of railway station architecture is most obvious in Enzensberger's favourite city, Oslo, where the opposition between the old and new railway stations is striking:

Oslo also has its bulldozer fantasies. Its latest triumph is the construction of a new railway station, a deep red box equipped with escalators that reminds one of airports in some Latin American capitals. But here, too, the indestructible, laid-back Oslo emerged victorious: the planners did manage to desolate a wide area, but the old east wing of the station with its dignified front, its cast-iron columns and its classical construction of steel and glass had to be left untouched.

(1987: 261)

These comments on railway stations are not mere nostalgia praising older forms of architecture. They refer, in a paradigmatic manner, to the very heart of his microscopic art of reading both the city-text and the railway-text politically (Ferguson 1988; Azaryahu 1990). The paradigm of this sort of reading politically, Walter Benjamin's *Passagen-Werk* (1983) is mentioned when Enzensberger speaks of houses in Budapest (1987: 140; 1989a: 102).

My nominalist conception regards politics from the viewpoint of two temporalising figures – politicisation and politicking. The first opens a horizon for action; the second is operative within the horizon. Travelling is a situation likely to make people attentive to political aspects in diverse phenomena. These may, however, be experienced as a key to the dimensions of 'the political'. Language, space and time are quite obviously political, when read *à la* Enzensberger. With their help the spatial ordering of the polity and the temporal ordering of policy can be deconstructed, by demonstrating their dependence on the primary operations of politicking and politicisation.

8 Reading politically
National anthems as textual icons

Klaus Sondermann

In this chapter I read three national anthems (German, Finnish and Austrian) with a certain notion of the political. Although I refrain from entering into a wider discussion of the societal significance of this kind of text, I take the anthems to be apotheoses of 'the national'. By tracing the discursive construction of the nation analytically from 'space' to (supreme) 'being', I show that national anthems are a kind of textual icon. They are the embodiment of the nation in actual apotheotical events. The nation comes into existence through these particular acts – it 'is' only in such activities. At the same time, I show that the national anthem stands for something, namely for society (*societas*) understood as *Gemeinschaft* (*communitas*).

Reading national anthems politically, in my view, leads to the issues of politicisation, depoliticisation and sociation (i.e. the formation of 'society' – *Vergesellschaftung*). In this respect I have tried to show that 'the national' (that is, national anthems) is a major project to destroy or block 'the political'. 'The national' is so often a depoliticising construction.

THREE ANTHEMS: GERMANY, FINLAND, AUSTRIA

The Aryan does not attain full development within his own human qualities but rather in the extent of his preparedness to put all his capacities into the service of the *community* [*Gemeinschaft*]. The drive for self-preservation attains its noblest form in him when he freely subordinates his own individuality to the life of the *collectivity*, and, when the times require it, to make the supreme sacrifice . . . . Devoting one's own life to the *existence of the community* [*Gemeinschaft*] is the crowning glory of all ideas of sacrifice.

(Hitler 1933: 326–7)

To die for the fatherland is to live on.

(Cuban National Anthem)

The Tomb of the Unknown Soldier illustrates the macabre aspect of national conceptions and shows the nameless *Gemeinschafts*-citizen, the eternal Aryan who – deprived of all individuality – sacrifices his life for the community (*Gemeinschaft*) (Anderson 1988: 18). The three national anthems chosen here work in much the same way, displaying glorified triviality, 'the national' as pomp and kitsch (see Figures 8.1, 8.2 and 8.3).

1.	Deutschland, Deutschland über alles,	1.	Germany o'er all the others,
2.	Über alles in der Welt,	2.	O'er all that's in the world,
3.	Wenn es stets zu Schutz und Trutze,	3.	For security and pride it ever
4.	Brüderlich zusammenhält.	4.	Holds together fraternally.
5.	Von der Maas bis an die Memel,	5.	From the Meuse up to the Niemen,
6.	Von der Etsch bis an den Belt,	6.	From Adige to Baltic Sea,
7.	Deutschland, Deutschland über alles,	7.	Germany o'er all the others,
8.	Über alles in der Welt.	8.	O'er all that's in the world.
9.	Deutsche Frauen, deutsche Treue,	9.	German women, Germans true,
10.	Deutscher Wein und deutscher Sang,	10.	German wine and German song,
11.	Sollen in der Welt behalten,	11.	Shall keep before the world,
12.	Ihren alten schönen Klang.	12.	Their old renowned fame,
13.	Uns zu edler Tat begeistern,	13.	Shall move us to noble deeds,
14.	Unser ganzes Leben lang,	14.	All our livelong days,
15.	Deutsche Frauen, deutsche Treue,	15.	German women, Germans true,
16.	Deutscher Wein und deutscher Sang!	16.	German wine and German song!
17.	Einigkeit und Recht und Freiheit,	17.	Unity and Right and Freedom,
18.	Für das deutsche Vaterland!	18.	For the German fatherland,
19.	Danach laßt uns alle streben,	19.	Let us altogether struggle,
20.	Brüderlich mit Herz und Hand!	20.	Fraternally with heart and hand!
21.	Einigkeit und Recht und Freiheit,	21.	Unity and Right and Freedom,
22.	Sind des Glückes Unterpfand,	22.	Are good fortune's pledge,
23.	Blüh im Glanze dieses Glückes,	23.	Blossom in good fortune's splendour,
24.	Blühe deutsches Vaterland!	24.	Bloom forever fatherland!

Figure 8.1 The German National Anthem, 1841

1. Oi maamme, Suomi, synnyinmaa,	1. O our country, Finland, land of our birth,
2. Soi, sana kultainen!	2. Chime, golden word!
3. Ei laaksoa, ei kukkulaa,	3. No vale, no hill,
4. Ei vettä rantaa rakkaampaa,	4. No waters, no lake is more beloved,
5. Kuin kotimaa tää pohjoinen,	5. Than this northern homeland,
6. Maa kallis isien.	6. The precious country of our fathers.
7. Sun kukoistukses kuorestaan,	7. Your prosperity,
8. Kerrankin puhkeaa;	8. At last bursts into blossom;
9. Viel' lempemme saa nousemaan,	9. Your hope, your splendid joy,
10. Sun toivos, riemus loistossaan.	10. Makes our love rise.
11. Ja kerran laulus, synnyinmaa,	11. Land of our birth, your song,
12. Korkeemman kaiun saa.	12. Sounds the highest resonance.

Original Swedish version

Vårt land, vårt land, vårt fosterland,
Ljud högt, o dyra ord!
Ej lyts en höjd mot himlens rand,
Ej sänks en dal, ej sköljs en strand,
Mer älskad an vår bygd i nord,
Ån våra fäders jord.

Figure 8.2 The Finnish National Anthem, 1847

It is not, of course, musical content that endows such texts with so much political seriousness, statesmanlike solemnity and national (*völkischer*) emotion. These are texts in which even 'the most useful servants of civilising activity turn into fire-worshippers and confessors of blood myth' (Kraus 1989: 17). These are texts in which gaudy pathos and ridiculous pathology coincide. They belong rather to the determining criteria of 'the national': 'the nation' or 'the national' is to a large extent a solemn staging of rather odd ideas. 'The national', at least in the bourgeois post- and counter-revolutionary design, is often a campy apotheosis of trivial oddities. Glorification and worshipping – apotheoses – are barely possible without triviality. Apotheoses require triviality and turn easily into kitsch. The apotheoses of 'the national', as can be observed today, are accomplished by organising an enormous 'consumption of symbols, flags and fireworks' (Kraus 1989).

1. Land der Berge, Land am Strome,	1. Land of mountains, land of streams,
2. Land der Äcker, Land der Dome,	2. Land of fields, land of churches,
3. Land der Hämmer, zukunftsreich!	3. Land of foundries, future wealth!
4. Heimat bist du großer Söhne,	4. You are home to worthy sons,
5. Volk, begnadet für das Schöne,	5. People blessed for beauty's sake,
6. Vielgerühmtes Österreich!	6. Far renowned Austria!
7. Heiß umfehdet, wild umstritten,	7. Wars all round you, fiercely fought,
8. Liegst dem Erdteil du inmitten,	8. Centred in the Continent,
9. Einem starken Herzen gleich.	9. Like a sturdy heart.
10. Hast seit frühen Ahnentagen,	10. Since olden days of yore,
11. Hoher Sendung Last getragen,	11. Burdened with the highest calling,
12. Vielgeprüftes Österreich!	12. Well proved Austria!
13. Mutig in die neuen Zeiten,	13. Courageous towards the future,
14. Frei und gläubig sieh uns schreiten,	14. See us free and faithful go,
15. Arbeitsfroh und hoffnungsreich.	15. With joy in work and filled with hope.
16. Einig laß in Brüderchören,	16. Let us sing as one fraternity,
17. Vaterland, dir Treue schwören,	17. Swearing loyalty to the fatherland,
18. Vielgeliebtes Österreich!	18. Much beloved Austria!

Figure 8.3 The Austrian National Anthem, 1947

Thailand is the incarnation of all the blood and flesh of the Thai race.

Thailand for the Thais.

(Thai National Anthem)

NUMINOUS QUALITIES OF IMAGINED SPACES

In some of my research I suggest that national *Vergemeinschaftung* or 'community building', which forms one of the basic elements in all xenophobic and xenophile phenomena, should be explored not only as a problem of attitudes, rights and policies, but should also be interrogated with a distinct notion of 'the political'. My research interests (which are normally assigned to migration research, aliens policy, racism, etc.) are for this reason concentrated on an examination of the way that exclusive–inclusive practices in 'the national' block 'the political'. This requires me to put forward different conceptions of the way that 'the national' is constructed. One of these deals with apotheoses of 'the national' in which numinous qualities become apparent.

> Whatever form they take, the symbols for a collectivity in all its aspects – symbols which fire up the emotional connections between individuals and the collectivity – these symbols themselves appear to be composed of peculiar qualities; these qualities, so to say, lend the collectivity a numinous existence in itself, over and against the individuals who form it – a kind of holiness, as previously ascribed to supernatural beings. It is a distinguishing sign of the democratic process, which has perhaps not yet come to attention, that in the course of this process people attach such numinous qualities and corresponding emotions to the society [*Gesellschaft*] which they themselves form with one another.
>
> (Elias 1989: 189–90)

From space to being

There are different ways to imagine the nation, the fatherland, the native country. There are different techniques of discursive construction utilised to persuade people to believe in their own nation. The regions, countries, nations, nation-state, *in* which we live, are often expressed in the rhetoric of everyday speech as a kind of space, or, more precisely, a container. In these containers things happen; things exist, enter and leave. Everyday discourse about the nation-state is expressed in metaphors which construct space discursively in the form of containers. In these different, more or less sharply distinguished terraria there are sub-divisions, sub-containers, fields and areas. Politics has its own field or space, its own national region, inhabited by a tribe of politicians. These spaces are furnished with different attributes, both ephemeral and long-lasting. The nation is a container with a pronounced tendency to stability.

The nation-container, however, undergoes metamorphoses of different kinds. It becomes an active space which forms an acting subject which may live or die. It becomes a partner in communication which then relates to other living spaces. In short, the nation-container turns into a 'being' (Sondermann 1992).

One particular metamorphosis can be observed in the Baltic states. The Estonian parliament passed a new nationality act (in February 1992). All 'Estonians' recognised as such from the time of the first period of independence (1918–40) and their descendants automatically receive Estonian citizenship (following *jus sanguinis*). All others (mainly Russian-speaking people), even if they were born in Estonia (not following *jus soli*), must (a) wait two years, (b) demonstrate knowledge of the Estonian language, and (c) take an oath of allegiance to 'Estonia' (whatever this might be). (See the Austrian National Anthem, ll. 16–17, above). This shows two aspects of 'the national' in a single law: the nation as *Abstammungsgemeinschaft* (community by extraction) and as *Loyalitätsgemeinschaft* (community by loyalty). 'Aliens' must pledge allegiance and swear loyalty. Loyalty, however, is considered an innate attribute of ethnically pure citizens. 'The national' becomes a network of consanguinity in which impure blood ('un extraño enemigo' – Mexican National Anthem), as in the army or in marriage, can be joined in purity by an oath of loyalty – until death do you part! Swearing an oath is a common figure in national anthems, such as those of Albania, Algeria, Argentina, Belgium, Bolivia, Canada, Chile, Egypt, Ireland, Italy, The Netherlands, Peru, Saudi Arabia and Uruguay. Thus the human content of the container is conceived as an exclusive tribe, as *Gemeinschaft*, which – when personified – becomes an active subject. The living and – as the nation is always a necrophiliac practice – the dead are understood as the content of the terrarium, not as the social interaction of citizens. Rather, as Carl Schmitt (1993) points out, the nation is understood as a 'political unit', ultimately having the nature of a subject.

Sporting events, such as the Olympics, are a locus in which the numinous qualities of 'the national' come sharply to the fore. At the moment when the national anthem of the winner strikes up and the relevant flag slowly rises, the flush of victory – with waving flowers, laughing and celebration – breaks off. People stand at attention and turn, as in a religious ritual, towards the flag. The numinous qualities of the container, the worship of a supreme being, appear in this situation, because a 'pious soul senses God in the sublime fatherland' (Swiss National Anthem).

National anthems as icons, as apodictic and persuasive speech

Apotheotic rituals are often understood as marginal and rather petty, as a kind of folklore, which has little to do with political behaviour, and even less with the analysis of 'the political'. The nation, as extolled in anthems, is a holy 'super-individual unit given by God, the history of the world, and nature' (Stölting 1988: 201). It requires festive atmosphere, rites, costumes and scenery in appropriately permanent forms. However, it also requires the normality of ordinary everyday occurrence. The nation is not merely spectacle and ritual, it also manifests itself as triteness in order to ensure an identificatory representation. During the French Revolution, and for some time afterwards, this could still be understood as the 'general will', but viewed historically, we see that it was quickly turned into an embodied 'particular will' by 'political' leaders.

I have looked into some aspects of this normality to see where 'the public' is and how *Vergesellschaftung* ('sociation') happens, namely in the public space represented by newspapers (Sondermann 1992; also Pietilä and Sondermann 1994). In this study I proceeded from the assumption that the discursive construction of foreigners can only be understood in and through the components of so-called identity in nationalised subjects. Forms of activity that exclude are not only societal or state-bureaucratic acts, they originate and are tied to the daily production of meaning. 'Excluding practices' are bound together with 'including practices' of normality, and hence to common binary distinctions. Strangers are 'others' and are the 'excluded group which represents the opposite virtues by which the identity community is distinguished' (Hall 1989: 919).

> The inhabitants of Sirius are not wholly alien to us – at least not in the sense of the word that comes into consideration in sociology – rather they do not exist in a general sense for us, they stand somewhere beyond the far and near. 'The other' is an element of the group itself.
>
> (Simmel 1987: 63)

So-called 'identity', which as national or cultural identity occupies a central place in complex conjunctions of ideological activities, shows the power of these constructions particularly well. The general, 'naturally' understood requirement to be for the fatherland or the like, without involving personal interests or welfare, is based on one argument (among others) that requires us to disregard individual interests. It is founded on the assertion that there is something like a specific national identity, which can be distinguished from others' identities. This identity is a *Gemeinschaftlichkeit* (*esprit de corps*), which differentiates and discriminates subjects of one nation-state from those of other nation-states. It is received without making a deliberate decision 'naturally' from society. It is difficult to resist a national identity – especially if it is *völkisch* constructed – because it belongs to the citizen in just the way that she or he is a mammal. National identity is a symbolically constructed coercive collective, and it is always tendentially and latently depoliticising – it narrows the space for action, and blocks alternatives.

In apotheoses everyday national identity is invoked in order to appeal to the emotions and to get emotional reactions. One should, in my view, be even more cautious in applying the notion of symbolic construction to apotheoses than to national identity. National anthems, to be sure, conform to some of the essential characteristics of symbols – iconism, motivating qualities, ambiguity, etc. – but there is something specific in the way that they function as icons. If we take a typical example of a symbol, namely the Bastille (Lüsenbrink and Reichardt 1990), then we find a concrete site (a prison, razed in 1789) in which a political regime was materialised, so to speak, and which merged by extension with various associated concepts – despotism, liberation, conquest and revolutionary action. The Bastille thus forms an icon; it is something and stands for something.

National anthems and similar apotheoses of 'the national' embody a somewhat stricter or more radical iconism, an iconism that is dissociated somewhat more from 'standing for something'. The national anthem is the nation in the concrete social situation of the apotheotical event. 'The national' comes into being through these particular acts – it 'exists' somehow only in such activities. At the same time, the national anthem stands for something, namely for society (*societas*) understood as *Gemeinschaft* (*communitas*). The anthem is thus a situation in which the 'Commune Sanctorum' is the 'Cummunio Sanctorum' and represents it. In other words, the texts of these national anthems somehow combine presence and distance; they speak to the being they build. One could understand the 'production' of the numinous qualities of 'the national' in a similar way. For example, the change from *noli me tangere* as a way of resisting feudal power to a modern declaration of sacrifice – giving up 'one's own life for the continued existence of the community' – somehow requires 'the national' as an already existing numinous being. And it also '(re-)produces' the numinous quality of the *Gemeinschaft* in such an expression.

In this respect I take national anthems – although I neglect the musical aspects – at their word. They are 'the national'. From a semiotic point of view, this is surely an arbitrary definition of the iconism exemplified in national anthems, which I combine, probably arbitrarily again, with two notions from rhetoric. In my view national anthems are – politically read or societally understood – simultaneously apodictical and epideictic speeches. They are apodictical, unlike the meaning in classical rhetoric, not because conclusions are deduced from syllogisms of indisputable premises, but because social convention and the law protect their numinous quality. The apodictical, the indisputable, also refers to the concrete act of staging, in which objections to iconic and numinous qualities of the *Gemeinschaft* are not permitted.

But national anthems are also epideictic in that they are supposed to persuade. They persuade in the concrete act of nation-building, and they celebrate the *Gemeinschaft*. Understood in this way, I will take the three anthems at their word and read them politically, that is, with regard to politicisation/depoliticisation/sociation.

TEXTS OF THREE NATIONAL ANTHEMS

Germany (text: Hoffmann von Fallersleben 1841; melody: Joseph Haydn) *is* Central Europe – from the Meuse to the Niemen, etc. (ll. 5/6), which contains fraternal solidarity (l. 4). For this solidarity the brothers require necessary drugs, namely German women, German wine and the German choral society, which enthuse them to noble deeds (ll. 9/10/13). The German anthem is a product of German nationalism, which borrows phrases from the Enlightenment and the French Revolution, phrases that are no longer related to the free individual, but to the excluding *Gemeinschaft* of 'the nation'. The German national anthem was written in 1841, that is, less than thirty years after the so-called 'Wars of Liberation' (1813–15), in which liberation from the Napoleonic army also brought liberation from the idea of personal freedom. This was just thirty years before the violent founding of the Second Reich.

Finland (text: Johann Ludwig Runeberg [Swedish] 1847; Paavo Kajander [Finnish]; melody: Friedrich Pacius) is the fathers' precious country (l. 6), composed of agriculturally, horticulturally and pisciculturally used space, and belongs only to native Finns. The

Finnish anthem is the solemn construction of an *Abstammungsgemeinschaft* (land of our birth, country of our fathers) combined with a naturalisation of social relations.

The Austrians (text: Paula von Preradovic; melody: W.A. Mozart) are a 'people of glorious sons, who swear together in fraternal chorus' (ll. 4/16/17). Professing a rustic Catholicism and tourist industry, Austria extends along the Danube via Saint Anthony and then across potato fields into St Stephen's Cathedral. The Austrian national anthem, with its three verses, is textually and aesthetically the most impertinent, compared with the other examples. It includes all the attributes of the other anthems – naturalisation, blood relations, self-praise, exclusive masculinity, etc. – and represents the infantile worshipping of the nation.

Who, to whom, by what – ethos, pathos, logos

The style, or more accurately, the tone of the anthems is most easily compared with prayer – 'O Lord', 'Oi maame', 'Suomi', 'vielgeliebtes Österreich' – in which speech to or dialogue with the imagined being, 'the nation', differs only in nuance from addressing the deity. The Finnish anthem begins rather like a longing, homesick (monologic) lament of an emigrant and then turns, in the second verse, into a declaration of love for the land of birth. The Austrian remains the most constant in the distance between the voice (the speaker – 'we') and the addressee (Austria – 'you'); it speaks to all Austria as an audience. The German anthem, in wavering between 'praising the Lord' and 'we' the congregation, concentrates more on the *Gemeinschaft* of the parishioners.

These three anthems, like many others as well, have in common a transposition in 'the speaker'. They shift from talking to the addressee (you, 'the nation') to a collective monologue (we, the *Gemeinschaft*); they speak to a being external to the singer and also speak as a 'we-choir'. This appears very evidently in one passage of the German anthem, in which the 'basis of linguistic expression, the correctness of language' (Aristoteles 1980) is violated: 'For security and pride it ever/Holds together fraternally' (ll. 3/4). As we do not suppose that Germany is schizophrenic, this leaves us wondering how the singular being 'Deutschland' is able to hold together 'fraternally' – it talks to the being, it is the being. The *Gemeinschaft* the singers form is at the same time a being one can talk to. The nation appears in this transposition of the speaker as the (supreme) being which citizens form themselves. The division of attributes or tasks

Germany	*We, the nation*	*You, the nation*
	Holds together fraternally	O'er all that's in the world
	Shall move us to noble deeds	German wine and German song/Shall keep before the world/Their old renowned fame
	All our livelong days	Unity and right and freedom/ For the German fatherland
	Let us altogether struggle	Blossom in good fortune's splendour
	Fraternally with heart and hand!	Bloom forever fatherland!

Figure 8.4 Germany

Finland	*We, the nation*	*You, the nation*
	Our country	Land of our birth
	. . . is more beloved/Than this homeland	(No) vale, hill, waters, lake
	Makes our love rise	The precious country of our fathers
	Sounds the highest resonance	Bursts into blossom
		Your hope, your splendid joy
		Your song

Figure 8.5 Finland

given to the (supreme) being and to the *Gemeinschaft* demonstrate this rhetorical strategy (see Figures 8.4, 8.5 and 8.6).

Austria	We, the nation	You, the nation
	People blessed for beauty's sake	Land of mountains, streams, fields, churches, foundries
	Bold, free and faithful	Future wealth!
	With joy in work and filled with hope	Home to worthy sons
	Let us sing as one fraternity	Far renowned
	Swearing loyalty	Like a sturdy heart Well proved Much beloved

Figure 8.6 Austria

Space

The space of the nation in national anthems is a living space. It is composed of immovable objects, which can yet be animated. The German national anthem defines the national container rather generously as a linguistic cultural space, not much concerned with state borders and delimited only by the 'eternal' geography of nature (rivers, the sea). The Finnish nation-state, which has just officially celebrated its seventy-fifth birthday (1992), takes the post-glacial geographic formation of the Finnish landscape as its space. The Austrian nation is a container filled with nature and architecture, which is located 'like a sturdy heart' in Europe's body. The space of these nations is given by nature – not by organic transitory nature – but by 'eternal', beloved geographical formations. In the Finnish and the Austrian anthems in particular we find a characteristic naturalisation, which can also be observed in racist discourses, namely the naturalisation of social relations. This space of the nation is anything but political, precisely because it is characterised as 'eternal' and 'natural'.

Time

An everlasting floweret in dangerous weather.

> (Icelandic National Anthem)

Time in national anthems conforms to the concept of 'homogenous and empty time' (Benjamin 1969: 276; see also Anderson 1988). It becomes calendric time arising in the past and extending, in a way, right through the present into a future of still more tradition. The nation extolled in the anthems is either very old or eternal; it comes from 'olden days of yore' (Austria: l. 10), and is created out of a landscape which is thought to have been unchanged since prehistoric times and enjoys 'renown' through the ages.

The time of the nation does not know any turns or ruptures; it has no content. Nations, which are indubitably a phenomenon of modern times, are said to go back to the dawn of history, then to go forth into an era of unlimited duration, and to embark on a future that is traditional in substance. The time of the nation transforms the mere accident of belonging to an imagined *Gemeinschaft* into Destiny. The time of the nation transforms contingency into meaning.

> The people [*Das Volk*] is a kind of . . . blood-filled unity, a purely organic flux from whose past man came forth, into whose 'future' – sharply demarcated by tradition – his children will enter. Such a conception of 'the people' [*Volkstum*] thus expels time from history, even expels history itself: it is space and organic destiny, nothing else; it is that 'true collective' whose basic presuppositions are to suppress the present discomforts of the class struggle as utterly superficial and ephemeral.
>
> (Bloch 1985: 97)

Gender

The gender of national anthems is masculine. The nation is fathers, sons and brothers; it is the fathers' land (Finland), it has sons (Austria), or it forms a kind of brotherhood (Germany). The nation is a soldierly *Gemeinschaft*, a patrimony and a mother for sons to protect. The nation of the anthems is partriarchal; it is a family with a masculine head, brave sons, beautiful and noble mothers, and a family estate. This construction obviously reflects the so-called 'bourgeois morality' characteristic of the times in which these anthems were written, but it also bespeaks male concepts of ruling, as well as an apolitical, motherly harmony.

DEPOLITICISATION – SOCIATION

I shall close this chapter by returning to a discussion of 'the political'. As we can see, the texts of national anthems are characterised by an absence of alternatives, elimination of contingency, naturalisation of society, strategies of exclusion, we-constructions (*communitas*), etc. What does this mean for the notion of the political?

In considering sociation (*Vergesellschaftung*) as reflected in 'the national' (*Vergemeinschaftung*), one of my conclusions is that this *Vergemeinschaftung* operates with an eternalising notion of *Gemeinschaft*, in order to prevent contingent society, the 'eternal flux and pulse', from appearing. Thus political action – that is, the possibility of alternative spaces or outcomes or decisions – is blocked by constructions of 'the national', which erase any underlying voluntarism. Let us look closer at sociation.

> Society [*Gesellschaft*] in its widest sense is obviously where many individuals interrelate. We consider sociation [*Vergesellschaftung*] at different levels and of different kinds, from the temporary unity of a little walk together up to the intimate unity of a family or of a guild of the middle ages. The particular motives and intentions without which sociation could never proceed, form – so to speak – the body, the *material* of the social process; formally the outcome of these motives and success of these intentions is precisely what calls forth an interrelation, a sociation amongst its constituents.
>
> (Simmel 1987: 43)

If we follow this notion of society, that is, if we understand society explicitly as *societas* and not as *communitas*, then national we-constructions as they appear in national anthems (and elsewhere) are of interest – particularly in conjunction with other discursive constructions built up from history, culture, nature, and further conceptions which are generally anti-contingency. These conceptions, of which 'the national' is an extreme example, are linked with strong anti-societal tendencies. The societal as interactive experience, as sociation, is a varied experience of ends, finality, counterfinality, contingency, discrimination, a-sociation, failure, etc. Included in this understanding of the societal is a model of the political: continuous contingency in decision situations. In a sharp polemic and with heavy pathos Habermas calls upon his readers to defend *Gemeinschaft*.

> However, praise for unity, apologias for the contingent and the private, the celebration of discontinuity, difference and the moment, the rebellion of the periphery against the centre, the demands of the extraordinary against triviality – all this will not

allow us to evade the problems which, though general, could only be solved cooperatively with the last drops of a solidarity that is nearly bled dry.

(Habermas 1990: 16)

Yet he also polemicises on behalf of *Gemeinschaft* – 'For security and pride it ever/holds together fraternally' (German National Anthem: ll. 3/4) – against the political. The national anthems that I have attempted to read politically are an example of the depoliticising strategy in discursive constructions of 'the national'. I consider 'the national' as it appears today to be a 'project' to destroy or block the *citoyen* ideal. National anthems are depoliticising and anti-societal.

9 Invention and community
Hermeneutic politics in Europe

Josef Bleicher

PROLOGUE

The Single European Act brought in its wake a new entity, the 'European Community'. This chapter considers the 'European Community' as a symbolic construct, and as such entangled in a continuous interpretive process involving contestation, negotiation, reformulation, etc. Given that the status of this entity is undetermined (indeterminable?), it provides an ontological parallel to the epistemological uncertainties given expression within the 'new interpretive methodologies'.

Applying a hermeneutic approach to these concerns leads me to stress the 'situatedness' of interpretations of 'Europe' and 'Community'. 'Europe' and 'Community' come to be seen as discursive objects constructed in particular discursive practices that are established and enacted from within specific sites (political cultures, interest groups, etc.).

In order to consider the complex nature of these constructions, this chapter moves towards the rehabilitation of 'invention' as a methodologically relevant approach within hermeneutics. Trying to rescue it from the taint of falsity and fabrication it acquired in the sphere of symbolic constructions, I argue that the European Community can be and is 'invented' differentially. Social scientists attuned to new methodologies can attend to these inventions by providing contextualising interpretations of them – while also recognising that they, too, are implicated as inventors of a possible European future.

INTRODUCTION

> There is no such thing as objective truth about such a many-sided phenomenon as the EC anyhow: so anybody has the right to participate in the information process, but everybody also has a duty to know the basic facts.
>
> (Galtung 1973: 147)

These words were written twenty years ago when the EC still represented a fairly clear-cut entity. Soon after, with the first enlargement, its direction was less certain, being somehow located between a 'common market' and a nascent political entity. Today, after Maastricht, the picture is far less clear and the pursuit of an 'objective truth' about the EC even less promising.

This complication on the level of reality has been paralleled on the level of methodology. However one describes the shift away from homogeneity towards the heterogeneity of life-worlds – and the reign of the qualifier 'post-' offers a range of examples – these processes seem to have found their expression in our understanding of the processes of social scientific research. Ranging from Luhmann's (1990) radical constructivism to Garfinkel's ethnomethodology and cognitivist micro-sociology, for example, the questions pursued are now less often framed in terms of 'why?' than in terms of 'how?' Increasingly they are concerned more with discursive practices of reality creation than with a non-reflexive attempt to represent a pre-given reality 'out there'.

Galtung, quoted above, is of course also the author of the influential textbook *Theory and Method of Social Research*, and we can take his reference to 'process' as a starting point for methodological considerations in relation to the study of the formation of a 'European Community'.

HERMENEUTICS AND 'NEW INTERPRETIVE METHODOLOGY'

'New' as applied to methodology may stand here for location in the era of the 'post-', from post-positivist to postmodern, i.e. the recognition of the general and unavoidable interpretive nature of any form of enquiry, whether it is guided by an explicit method or not.

One of the results of escaping from the strait-jacket of positivist methodology is the acceptance of syncretism as not only legitimate but also necessary. That is to say, the pluralism in relation to 'method' is not just an epistemologically naive opting out of rigorous research procedures, but rather derives from the multi-dimensionality of the 'object'. This, in turn, relates to a pluralism on the level of lived experiences, or hermeneutic 'situatedness'. Formulated from the vantage point of agents, it is the fragmentation of social life – or the loss of community in postmodern times – that engenders differing ways of seeing and thereby differing constructions of the object.

In this sense, 'new' might also denote that we recognise the operation of the 'hermeneutic circle' as both the precondition and modus of understanding; and if 'hermeneutic' is allowed to stand as one specification of the 'new', then some of the following tenets would apply in the formulation of a 'new methodology':

1 The quest for a 'method' itself would have to be problematised. Following one author, it would be more appropriate to argue that 'the methodological framework is . . . an intellectual template for a movement of thought' (Thompson 1990: 291) rather than a fixed set of principles and directives. Furthermore, one would accept that there can be no a priori method formulated in abstraction of the object.

2 There would have to be an interrelation of interpretation, understanding, application in a triadic process that mediates past, present and future; researcher and object; the question and the answer; truth and method. 'Meaning' as dialogical and processual leads away from a concern with referentiality towards the activity of making sense, so consequently there would be a rejection of essentialism in favour of multi-dimensionality and a concern with the discursive constitution of the object. Foucault's denial of 'hermeneutic depth' would not necessarily conflict with this view, since it applies to an objectivistic hermeneutics to which I do not subscribe, i.e. one that does not fall within the ambit of the 'new'. Foucault's statement that there are 'always multiple layers or surfaces to be accounted for, none of which have the final say' (1986c: 3) is the one argued for here.

3 A 'new methodology' as a hermeneutically informed approach to the interpretation of symbolic constructs should also be able to provide a self-reflexive account of the conditions of its own possibility and practice.

'EUROPEAN COMMUNITY' AS 'OBJECT OF DISCOURSE'

'Community' forms the precondition for the hermeneutic experience. 'Dialogue', 'understanding', 'language', 'tradition' and especially 'consensus' – these core concepts refer us to some element of sharedness, to commonality, to community. In this way, the hermeneutic experience and community define and sustain one another: neither is possible without the other, and the one enriches the other.

In Gadamer's *Wahrheit und Methode*, however, *Gemeinschaft* does not even appear in the index. Where there is reference to the bond that makes social coexistence possible, it is at the beginning of the book where Gadamer outlines the importance of the humanistic tradition. It is with reference to Vico's work that Gadamer discusses not community as such but the *sensus communis*: 'What gives our will its direction, according to Vico, is not the abstract generality of Reason but the concrete generality formed by the commonality of the group, the people, the nation, or the whole of humanity' (1975: 1). And he continues by stating that 'the formation of this shared sense [con-sense] is of crucial significance in life' (1975: 18).

In relation to a 'European' community, we could ask to what extent a 'European spirit', 'identity' and 'community' have developed and can develop. However, this topic would lead us directly into an account of the plurality of political cultures in Europe, which is outside the scope of this chapter. What is pursued here is 'Europes' from different vantage points, so what is at issue, then, is the view expressed by Benedict Anderson: 'Communities are to be distinguished, not by their falsity/genuineness, but by the style in which they are imagined' (1991: 6).

This conception seems to be in line with the concerns of a 'new methodology', eschewing the meta-narrative of the 'real', the 'true' and the 'objective', in short the 'essence' of community.

'INVENTION' AS 'DISCURSIVE PRACTICE'

> European community action cannot move forward through established institutions but must create and consolidate its own; it has no well-defined political alternative expressed in definite political parties but must find them; it does not even have a political language of its own already formed but must *invent* one.
>
> (Spinelli 1966: 9)

What is the meaning of 'invention' here? Can it mean more than its usual sense of fabrication associated with falsehood? The point

James Sheehan makes in a very perceptive essay applies to the
European Community as well:

> To say that nations are invented does not mean that they are
> unreal or fictitious . . . nations are products of history and
> therefore are invented . . . as people discover and create the
> bonds of their nationality. Moreover, much of what is considered
> to be discovery turns out, upon closer examination, to have been
> created.
>
> (Sheehan 1985: 4)

As this paper aims to rehabilitate 'inventing' as an interpretive
mode of appropriation and construction of symbolic objects such
as 'Europe' and 'community', it may be of use to engage in some
clarification of the term itself and introduce some distinctions.

In the *Concise Oxford Dictionary* one finds: 'invent' *v.t.* 'create by
thought, originate, (new method, instrument, etc.); concoct (false
story etc.)'. This characteristic tension in its semantic meaning is
not only apparent in English usage. In Latin, the noun *inventum*
means 'invention, discovery, contrivance' (*Langenscheidt's Latin
Dictionary*). The German for 'invention', *erfinden*, provides a similar account (cf. *Duden's Deutsches Universalwörterbuch*):

1 to bring about something new through research and experiment
   esp. in field of technology
2 to make up something unreal or untrue.

The counter-positioning of these two strands of meaning, especially
in the German case, seems to reflect the 'two cultures' argument,
with truth value being assigned to creation in the sphere of nature,
while 'invention' in the cultural realm is characterised by distortion
and falsehood. Related terms give a similarly unflattering account
for the 'cultural' side: *concoct* – make up of mixed ingredients; *con-
trive* – find, imagine; also *contrivance* – deceitful practice, invention.

An attempt at mediating the two poles – truth and falsity, deceitful and genuine, real and concocted, honest invention and false fabrication – would start with a recognition that this polar
oppositioning is itself an invention, and that the tensions it establishes between the poles are always and already contained within the
terms themselves. That is to say, creative originality and deceptive
concoction are limiting cases of the process of discovery, whether in
common-sense accounts or methodologically guided research. All
interpretive activity involves us in inventing the object, by 'finding'
it in a particular way. The object is never available to us in a pristine

form 'out there' but is made available to us through the way we approach it.

Returning to the German rendition of the term and modifying it slightly provides us with the following insight: *er-finden* – the process of inventing – involves an active appropriation of the object, the meaning of which thereby becomes established in the triadic form indicated above (Gadamer 1975: 290–3; Bleicher 1980: 124–6). Invention as 'finding' moves between the poles of fraudulent fabrication and original creation, false and true; it also can be directed forward or backward in time. Within the field of force thus established between false and true, past and future, this chapter singles out the following modes through which to invent the European Community:

1   fabricating it (in the Latin sense of 'to frame, forge, construct, build', as a 'constructing' that is also a forging);
2   finding its roots of the present in the past through a process of retrojective invention;
3   reinventing it, i.e. finding in the past an image of the future;
4   rediscovering it as a creative appropriation;
5   imagining it as a projective finding of a reality-yet-to-be.

Fabricating the community: from simulation to simulacrum

The non-existence or impossibility of community is a central topos in post-structuralist writing. In Baudrillard's analysis (1988: 207–19) 'the masses' fill the place on the social map once occupied by 'community'. (Passive) TV culture relates to 'the mass' as (participatory) popular culture used to relate to living communities: the one presupposing and sustaining the other. In the era of simulated reality, and of the 'terrorism of the code', the mass is bombarded by an excess of information presented in a way that precludes a critical response – and thereby forms itself as that amorphous body, the mass. The mass occasions, and is occasioned by, 'the implosion of the social in the media'; it forms a 'black hole', sucking in shared meaning, and, with it, even the preconditions for communication. To follow Baudrillard's successive phases of the image, and the emergence of the 'hyperreal', we have now reached a stage in which the image 'bears no relation to any reality whatever: it is its own pure simulacrum', the latter having been defined by its source in *Ecclesiastes* as 'the truth which conceals that there is none' (Baudrillard 1988: 166–84). In this vein, fabricating inventions of

'Europe' and European identity or community serves only to hide the truth that no such thing does or can exist. Is it the absence of a real *sensus communis* that gives rise to the feverish attempts to establish one 'from above'?

It is not surprising that some of these attempts remain close to public relations and advertising techniques, not just in form but also in content. Current schemes, for example, include the following: the European flag to be displayed 'at the Community's external borders, at official events, on ships and as an emblem on car number plates'. Then there is Europe's contribution to Olympic Year 1992 . In view of the historical ties linking the Olympic ideals with the European cultural heritage, Parliament proposed that the year be declared European Olympic Year and that steps be taken to identify member states' athletes as belonging to 'Europe'.

The invention of 'Europe' as fabrication by interested groups, here the European Commission speaking 'for Europe' and taking 'the Community point of view', resembles earlier constructions of 'community', i.e. the 'nation' – if we define the nation, with Talcott Parsons, as the 'societal community'. Were one to push the analogy between Community and nation-building a bit further, then the *communitaire* projection of the European Community would be akin to the ideological function of nationalism. In Gellner's catchy phrase, 'Nationalism is not the awakening of nations to self-consciousness: it *invents* nations where they do not exist' (1964: 169).

The use of 'invention' here as the ideological projection of a nation is in contrast to the affirmation of a real community. In its adherence to notions of truth and falsity, genuine and fake, Gellner's usage is paralleled by writers with a similar epistemological self-certainty.

Retro-invention

Where Gellner is concerned with the projective, inventive fabrication of nations, Hobsbawm fleshes out this process in relation to the retrojective 'invention of tradition'. What both trajectories of invention share is the ideological definition accorded to 'invention', i.e. as the formulation of false claims in the interest of self-legitimation. Thoroughly pre-postmodernist, the editors of *The Invention of Tradition* appear epistemologically confident enough to refer to a 'past, real or invented' (Hobsbawm and Ranger 1983: 2). That they relate this process to some variant of the 'dominant ideology thesis' becomes equally clear in the opening statement in which invented traditions 'seek to inculcate certain values and norms' (Hobsbawm and Ranger 1983: 1), and at a later point when it is stated that they rest on exercises in social engineering which are often deliberate.

It is not intended here to deny validity to Gellner's and Hobsbawm's use of 'invention' but merely to draw attention to the point pursued, that invention as ideology represents only one moment in the hermeneutic appropriation of the object.

To widen the parameters of retro-invention beyond the inventive fabrication of tradition, it could be stated, with a certain exaggeration no doubt, that the retrojective 'finding' of Europe leads to the positing of essentialist notions of Europeanness.

Almost as a throwback to well-rehearsed modes of self-invention, European identity is often invented through the retrojective move of 'finding' its roots at the beginnings of 'European history'. The sources most frequently arrived at involve the 'seedbed' societies of ancient Israel and Greece. Inventions of Europe as Christendom and as the cradle of democracy, together with the stress on the individual and moral responsibility, continue this strand even today – but in a self-conscious way that cannot hide a trace of unease about this laboured and artificial positing of the 'real' meaning of being European.

Are there fundamental values 'we' all share, roots we all draw on – from the civilisation of ancient Greece, to Roman law, to Christianity, to the humanism of the Renaissance, the individuation of the Reformation, the liberalism announced in the French Revolution, the principle of self-determination of Romantic nationalism . . . ? Hagen Schulte (1990) even refers us back to the organisational structures of the Holy Roman Empire.

Retro-invention does not find a pristine past, however. It *erfindet* its object. Bernard Lewis recognises this, but goes on to state that

> [it] is perfectly natural and normal that the questions which an historian puts to the past are those suggested to him by the events of his own time. . . . What is improper is when the concerns of his own time suggest not only the questions but also the answers.
>
> (Lewis 1975: 98)

A hermeneutic approach adds the modification that the answers elicited depend themselves on the questions that were asked, i.e. how they opened up the dialogue with the past as text. This way of considering retro-invention as the *erfinden* – or finding a possible future for Europe, sought in a European past – has in fact been anticipated by Lewis. He pithily remarks in relation to the invention of the Roman Empire as Christian that '[A] new future required a different past'. Lewis draws attention to the discovery of the True Cross by St Helena, mother of the Emperor Constantine, which is still known as 'inventio crucis' (1975: 11).

It is worth noting that the retro-invention of a European essence cannot avoid dis-inventing aspects less appealing in the European heritage – even though they may well have been more effective historically. That is to say, retrieving a Golden Age of classical antiquity is predicated on the absence of other contributions made by Greek culture, such as tyranny and slavery, which unfortunately represent another Europeanness, one more familiar to non-Europeans. As one challenging work among many, see Stuart Miller's (1988) polemical counterblast to smug notions of the superiority of European civilisation.

At the same time, just as nation-building involved the 'boundary problem' familiar to cultural anthropologists, the invention of a European 'community', too, will be likely to adhere to Renan's view concerning the dis-invention of differences, i.e. that 'l'essence d'une nation est que tous les individus aient beaucoup de choses en commun, et aussi que tous aient oublié bien des choses' (quoted in Anderson 1991: 6, n. 10).

Reinventing as 'conjuring up'

A significant feature of discursive practices in Britain concerning 'Europe' which has come to the fore since 1990 revolves around the demonification of 'Germany'. It erupted onto the political scene in consequence of Nicholas Ridley's interview in the *Spectator* and a meeting of experts at Chequers, on the invitation of the Prime Minister, Margaret Thatcher, to discuss the question, 'Can we trust the Germans?' The wider context of these two spectacular manifestations of British – or should it just be 'English', as a body of Scottish opinion would insist – concerns can be adumbrated with reference to the transformation of Europe. From external events such as German unification and the collapse of communism, and events in the Gulf and Yugoslavia, to the push for a 'deepening' of Europe and the loss of 'sovereignty' this entails, together with internal dynamics such as continuing economic decline and separatist demands – all these and other considerations seem to have shaken not only the confidence of the political class in Britain but that of ordinary members of the public as well.

Without wanting to fill in this crude and schematic overview here, what is important for a discussion of the invention of 'Europe' is the recourse to old formulae and the symbolic strategies and discursive practices that this entails. In particular, I would point to the reifying construction of the motivation and 'character' of a group of people and to the process of making the similar appear different (dissimulation) and the different the same (unification) – Thompson (1990) outlines these 'modes of operation of ideology', such as legitimation, dissimulation, unification, fragmentation, reification. The move of likening Kohl to Hitler, and then the talk of the coming of the Fourth Reich from the Baltic to the Balkans, was made legitimate in political discourse in Britain by politicians, media figures and even intellectuals, particularly those with media roles.

The 'Europeanisation' of this particular symbolic construction as a retro-invention of 'Germany' is again a topic outside the scope of this chapter. That this 'finding' of the future in the past in the form of drawing parallels is not restricted to external commentators on 'the German problem', i.e. its potential dominance over Europe and attempts by others to counter it, can be seen from, for example, Helmut Schmidt's (1991) sombre allusion 'that we may again come to be in a position as it existed in the times of Victoria or Bismarck and Wilhelm II'. Similar worries, retro-inventions, can be noticed in the USA in relation to Japan, with Pearl Harbor serving as a trope in the depiction of a renewed menace from Japan and the perceived need to combat it. Its symbolic re-enactment within American political culture conforms to processes well described by David Procter (1991).

In attempting an interpretation of this form of re-invention – a pathological reactivation of the past under the guise of learning from history – it is apposite to quote Marx at some length. In a celebrated account of French politics in *The Eighteenth Brumaire of Louis Bonaparte*, he states that

> [the] tradition of all the dead generations weighs like a nightmare on the brain of the living. And just when they seem engaged in revolutionising themselves and things, in creating something entirely new, precisely in such epochs of revolutionary crisis they anxiously conjure up the spirits of the past to their service and borrow from them names, battle slogans and costumes in order

to present the new scene of world history in this time-honoured disguise and their borrowed language.

(Marx 1978: 595)

Inventing as rediscovering

Inventions drawing on the past need not remain its captive, destined to recapitulate its mistakes. The past can provide resources for facing a new future in new ways – resources developed earlier when the time had not been ripe for them. Inventions of Europe as rediscovery could draw on sources from the Enlightenment to the immediate past, in particular on documents developed in contexts characterised by intra-European cooperation that began to enact commonality and saw its further development as of crucial significance for the progress of our civilisation. Documents arising out of the turmoil of World War II are of specific value here on account of the urgency and moral force that underlies them (Lipgens 1985; Voigt 1988).

Plans for a European union had already taken shape in the Second World War. Monnet, 'the father of Europe', had worked for the French Committee of National Liberation. When the Schumann plan was being drawn up, Monnet recounts that 'the plans I had discussed in 1943 . . . now came back to my mind. At the time they had been intellectual blueprints. . . . Now I rediscovered them – or rather, reinvented them in response to the need of the hour' (1978: 293).

This 'inventing' as 'finding' and rediscovery has deeper roots. Lowenthal (1985) points out that the 'Humanists conceived the revival of antiquity as creative obeisance'; for them, following Keith Thomas, 'An "inventor" was . . . a person who found something which had been lost . . . not one who devised a new solution unknown to previous generations' (1985: 84). Touraine has also noted a tendency to such inventions in the case of new social movements:

[T]he cultural models of the past are left floating in our society. . . . They may be latched onto by nostalgic groups hoping to *rediscover* the core of a lost civilisation, whether it be the idea of God or that of progress; these past cultural models are most often interpreted by the new social movements and particularly by critical action desirous of *rediscovering* a principle to replace the void created by a crisis.

(Touraine 1981: 97; my emphasis)

Imaginative invention

Invention as creative and innovative also has a place in constructions of 'Europe'. Engaging in Popperian 'bold conjecture', it tries to imagine structures and ways of living that may at best exist in embryonic form at the time. Rather like Ernst Bloch's 'day dreams', they combine imagination and rational thought. These inventions represent the hermeneutic principle of the 'anticipation of completeness' (or perfection), without which conceptions of a possible future for Europe would lack their orienting horizon.

Among these imaginative inventions, federalist conceptions act as guiding lights, or Max Weber's 'switchmen of history', setting the tracks at crucial junctions in the development of a European framework. Such creative notions are hardly ever a creation *ex nihilo* but are themselves hermeneutically situated. To employ an etymological approach once again: the German verb *schöpfen* suggests a creation out of something, having as one of its meanings the notion of 'drawing from', e.g. a well. The 'totally new and original' is a limiting concept, in politics no less than in the arts or science. Invention of something different through associating elements previously unconnected is the more prevalent mode of imagining the new.

Linked with the limited awareness that the author/inventor necessarily brings to the process of imaginative invention is the likelihood that the invention takes on a life of its own, as it were, bringing it within the realm of unintended consequences of action. Willy Brandt provides a telling example of this form of invention:

> As far as the EC is concerned, there have been some terribly wrong developments. I can recall the day when Jean Monnet came to see me; I was then Chancellor. We had invented this 'European Council', that now has failed so miserably in Athens, and we could not envisage what it turned into. It is now an instance of appeal. It was conceived of as the nucleus of a European government, always on the condition that the work of the Commission would not be hampered by it. At this moment, nothing fits properly anymore.
>
> (Brandt 1983)

The lack of fit bemoaned here directs attention to the possibility that we are seeing the emergence of an entity to which traditional structures and concepts no longer apply. Authors, such as Dahrendorf, have begun to accept the Europe beyond the twelve that is in the making as a reality *sui generis* (1990). Its relevant ingredients – from EC to EFTA, WEU, NATO, CWSCE, Council of Europe, to the various external links, often with a global reach, that member states bring into the 'mix' – are ascertainable and estimable; the way that economic, political, social and cultural dynamics and interests gel is clearly not. This void, while making for uncertainty, also frees the imaginative invention of a 'Europe' that is true to the best in its own history and responsive to the demands of an interdependent world. If nations are 'imagined communities', then the emergence of a post-national community requires imaginative, constructive forward-looking invention even more urgently.

CONCLUSION

A hermeneutic of invention participates in the postmodern epistemological shift from a concern with the truth content of statements to their mode of construction, to the 'how?' of the various inventions of a plurality of 'Europes' and 'Communities', rather than the 'what?'. On the basis of the interrelationship of object and methodology referred to at the beginning of this chapter, indeterminacy at both levels is mutually supportive in a hermeneutic framework.

In this light, one would even have to question Galtung's quoted exhortation to know the 'basic facts'. Considering the plurality of inventions and the diversity of political cultures that sustain them, the convergence of interpretation towards something 'factual' in the sense of 'uncontroversial' would be likely to come about either because the events concerned are trivial, i.e. not worth arguing about because differences are of no consequence, or in the sense of standing outside controversy because they rest on an a priori consensus in terms of shared conventions, e.g. historical dates.

Beyond this, making sense of events is a process taking various hermeneutic routes. The European Community as an object is many-sided, and disagreements deriving from political cultures need to be recognised as such before they can be dissolved, or at least approached, dialogically.

How may conflicts of inventions be dissolved and a European political culture be established? Can it be formulated substantively, or is it to be invented imaginatively using formal principles of conflict resolution, consensus formation and other processes that make social and societal coexistence possible and enriching? Can we conceive of a European way of life (Schwengel 1989) – or are we inescapably caught in a play of floating signifiers and without anchorage in anything real beyond crude power interests? Are the inventions through which we are trying to 'find our way' in an over-complex world ever more than a gloss on inexorable processes, on self-inventing realities and auto-poetic systems, within which 'Europe' and its 'Community' are merely transitory constellations in the globalised process of capital accumulation and quests for political dominance?

It may not be necessary to follow the postmodern road down to its nihilistic consequences. While the sociological underpinning of this approach – the fragmentation of community, collective and individual identity, etc. – is persuasive, the moral–cultural consequences to be drawn may be quite different. A lack of metanarrative certainty can be devastating and lead to nihilism; it can also be liberating, clearing the view ahead and requiring us to 'invent' our Europe in the light of our concerns and hopes: an *Erfindung* that eschews essentialism and 'timid traditionalism' and perhaps finds its roots in the future by using a form of hermeneutic imagination (Bleicher 1980).

'New methods for a new object' might be the motto. As Bernd Hamm put it succinctly:

> European integration, seen as the emergence of a new society, introduces a new quality and therefore requires a thorough revision of many aspects of the social sciences. The traditional approach – positivist, retrospective, cross-sectional, unidisciplinary, and allegedly value-free – is not adequate for understanding this process or even its important components. At the same time, the social sciences have an enormous task to fulfil: they are called upon to contribute to the shaping of this new society and of a humane transition process.
>
> (Hamm 1992: 19)

This imaginative invention would require of us a new way of thinking and speaking. As social scientists and members of this 'community-to-be' we are also inventors, cultural producers and interpreters (Bauman 1987). We have our own agenda revolving around the – self-interested – pursuit, for example, of freedom of expression and plurality. In the words of the previous Commissioner for Culture, Ripa di Meana, who formulated the invention of Europe entailed here very clearly: 'Europe's cultural identity is nothing less than a shared pluralistic humanism based on democracy, justice and freedom. Expressed in the diversity of our local, regional and national cultures, it is the basis for European Union' (1987).

Remembering, however, that we are also members of a community wider than the European Community, and eschewing the temptations of essentialism and Euro-centrism, we also have to invent ourselves anew. Given the tasks ahead, are we not still at the stage of Marx's 'beginner', who 'has assimilated the spirit of the new language and can produce freely in it only when he moves in it without remembering the old and forgets in it his ancestral tongue' (1978: 595)?

10 The simulation syndrome
From war games to game wars

James Der Derian

After the informational euphoria of 1989, the first week of February had the feel of a morning after. Media dealerships handed out bromides when President Mikhail Gorbachev yet again did the unthinkable, proposing an end to the Soviet Communist Party's monopoly on power. News junkies hardly twitched when President George Bush once more responded with the predictable, calling a five-minute time-out during a war game at Fort Irwin's National Training Center to let the soldiers know the good news. Kitted out in a photo-opportunistic ensemble of camouflage jacket, pin-stripe trousers and wing-tip shoes, Bush used a radio link to tell the 2,689 players spread out over the Mojave Desert that 'we are pleased to see Chairman Gorbachev's proposal to expand steps toward pluralism in the Soviet Union'. Inspired, the 'Soviet' 197th Krasnovian Motorized Rifle Regiment made bortsch out of the US Third Brigade of the Ninth Infantry Division, and then headed for the ridge from which Bush had pledged not 'to let down our guard against a worldwide threat'. But Bush – clearly impressed by the power of fictitious forces over real ones – had already left for a briefing tour of the Livermore Labs, birthplace and incubator of Star Wars.

Of course, making the unthinkable predictable is Bush's number one job. But is it a historical irony or just the dumbness of imperial decline that should suddenly make war games such an attractive diplomatico-strategic tool for the job?

Perhaps it is simply a matter of centennial coincidence. In 1889 Major William Livermore of the Army Corps of Engineers joined William McCarty Little and Rear Admiral Alfred Thayer Mahan at the Naval War College to set up the nation's first modern system of war gaming. Spurred by the success of the expansionist Prussians who had used *Kriegsspiel* ('war play') before their victories over the

Austrians at Sadowa in 1866 and the French in 1870, these early advocates of American war gaming found their positions strengthened when Japan achieved a stunning victory over the Russians in 1904 – a victory plotted out beforehand with newly created war games.

Long before Bush made his trip to the Mojave, war gaming had sallied from the battlefield, emerged from the basements of the war colleges, leaked out of the high-security rooms of research centres like RAND and BDM International, and entered, if not seized, the public imagination. One reason for the shift is the computerisation of war gaming. Just as the art of warfare has undergone radical changes, so too has the art of gaming. At the microchip level, the slow, spatial movement of toy soldiers and cardboard ships, the contoured sand tables and expansive game rooms have largely been replaced by the high-speed electronic calculations and high-resolution screens of computer simulations. And from their inception thirty years ago, computer war games have undergone radical changes. When the Naval War College finally closed down its old tiled war-gaming room in 1958, it was replaced with the Navy Electronic Warfare System (NEWS) which cost more than $10 million and filled a three-storey building. Today those very NEWS games could be played on the home computer.

And *they are* being played at home, as well as at the movies and in the classrooms. One of the most popular games, 'Balance of Power', requires only 256K memory, two disk drives and the introduction of Syria into any scenario to trigger World War III (personal best: two minutes to reach Armageddon). Almost every mall now has a video arcade full of remarkably sophisticated war games: one can fly as 'Top Gun', rescue hostages *successfully*, or win historical (and some not so historical) military conflicts. Many of the wildly popular 'Nintendo' games are based on military simulations. There is the film *War Games*, about a young hacker who taps into an Air Force computer and nearly triggers a nuclear war between the superpowers, which is currently enjoying high-volume sales and rentals as a video. And more recently Ted Koeppel assembled – 'for the first time ever' – a group of high-ranking military and government officials from the Soviet Union and the USA to play out a war game for an ABC prime-time audience.

Moreover, the war at home is increasingly being gamed. Before the 1984 Los Angeles Olympics, the various law enforcement agencies responsible for security got together to train for possible terrorist attacks. They took advantage of a new 'tactical mapping system' created by the United States Agency for Advanced Research Projects, which had put over 54,000 moving images of Aspen, Colorado, on instantly accessible videodiscs (a veritable mink farm for animal rights counter-terrorists?). In Los Angeles, likely building targets were similarly videotaped, down to the detail of door locks and ventilation systems. Anti-terrorist specialists then trained by 'walking through' computer simulations, their eyes becoming the camera's eye.

My purpose, however, is not simply to give notice of the computer diffusion of war games. Nor is it to claim that a pervasive militarisation of society is likely to result. That might be a possibility, but there is a more complex, if less obvious, danger that deserves our attention. The proliferation of simulations into all walks of life – as news (re)creations, video games, flight simulators, police interrogations and war plans – has weakened and in some cases displaced the representational boundary between the simulation and the 'real thing'.

We all have some notion of the reality of war, but just what is its simulation? It could be broadly defined as the 'continuation of war by means of verisimilitude'. Conventionally, a 'war game' uses broad descriptive strokes and a minimum of mathematical abstraction to make generalisations about the behaviour of actors, while the 'simulation' uses algorithms and computer power to analyse the amount of technical details considered necessary to predict events and the behaviour of actors. Judging by the gradual shift by the military and think-tanks from games to mainly computerised simulations – reflected in the shift of the Joint Chiefs of Staff gaming organisation from SAGA (Studies, Analysis, and Gaming Agency) to JAD (Joint Analysis Directorate) – it would seem that simulation is becoming the preferred, 'sponge' term. 'Simulation' also has the obvious advantage of sounding more serious than 'gaming' and of carrying more of a high-tech, scientific connotation than modelling. Driven by the goal of total authenticity and rendered by new scientific methods of reproduction, the war simulation is leading us into a brave new world. The writer J.L. Borges anticipated this realm in his fable about the cartographers who, when ordered by the emperor to draw the perfect map of the empire, created one that exactly and entirely covered the territory. The social critic Jean Baudrillard recounts this story to make a telling point: we now have the technical means to make maps and models that seem as real as the reality that they simulate. 'Virtual' or 'artificial' reality is what the computer scientists are calling it. Baudrillard refers to it as the realm of hyperreality, where origins are forgotten, referents lost and simulations begin to precede and engender reality. This is the world of Mutual Assured Destruction, Star Wars and stealth technology, all of them deterrence machines that most persuasively 'work' in the hyperreal world of strategic simulation (a point brought home by the botched bombing of the Panamanian military barracks by a stealth FB-117).

A hyperreal simulation can take on many forms. For the radar operator and the tactical information coordinator of the USS Vincennes on 3 July 1988 it looked like an attacking Iranian F-14, even though their highly sophisticated Aegis radar system registered an unidentified airplane flying level at 12,000 feet. Is it possible that the nine months of simulation training with computer tapes that preceded the encounter engendered a hyperreality which absorbed the reality of the moment? Did the Iranian Airbus, in effect, disappear before the surface-to-air missile struck, fading from a plane with 290 civilians to an electronic representation on a radar screen to a simulated target? Can a simulation overpower a reality which does not conform to it?

A later military investigation laid the blame on stress: the Vincennes and its crew had never been in combat, they were engaged with Iranian speedboats at the time, and surely the memory of the USS Start – which did not fire at an Iraqi warplane and was nearly sunk by an Exocet missile – was on everyone's mind. Yet stress has many origins, and the military shows signs of ignoring the most serious one: the tension that can develop when the simulation becomes too real.

Symptoms have appeared elsewhere in the armed services. Although the Air Force has thrown a veil of secrecy over it, the Army, Navy and Marine Corps have become alarmed by the sharp increase in cases of 'simulator sickness'. This is a condition in which users of flight simulators – especially those that make use of powerful computers to create the most 'realistic' motions and graphic representations of flight – experience flashbacks, visual distortions and physical disorientation. Experts are unsure of the cause, but many of them attribute the disorder to 'cue conflict', which happens when one's expectations based on experience run up against contrary sensory information.

Should we be on the alert against a similar effect taking hold in the ranks of military and diplomatic officials, as well with the international relations specialists, who create, play and promote war games? Is there sufficient evidence of a 'simulation syndrome' creeping into our infinite preparations for war as well as war-fighting itself?

Probably not. Certainly there is not sufficient proof to wean the Navy from its 'Global Game' or the Army from its 'Janus' game as their preferred training method. Or to deter the Foreign Service Institute from using simulations like the 'Crisis in Al Jazira' to educate junior-level diplomats in the art of crisis management and counter-terrorism. Or to prevent the ubiquitous think-tanks from modelling everything from domestic crime to nuclear war, and selling them to the highest bidder. In turn, we – the inhabitants of advance mediacracies – have become seduced by the technical reproduction of reality, especially its highest stage of development, the computer simulation. What will happen when the computer representation of reality moves into even more spectacular realms, where with the aid of holograms, interactive media, sensor helmets, data gloves and other technologies of virtual reality we can fully inhabit the cyberspace of a three-dimensional, computer-generated hyperreality?

We should probably turn to science fiction rather than social science – to *Bladerunner* and *Robocop*, William Gibson and other cyberpunk writers, or perhaps MIT's MediaLab – to find answers to such speculative questions. Indeed, the movie *Aliens* provides an eerie foreshadowing to the Vincennes incident. When the colonial marines are being buffeted as they enter the atmosphere of the planet where the Alien awaits them, Ripley (Sigourney Weaver) asks the obviously anxious lieutenant how many combat drops this is for him. He replies, 'Thirty-eight', pauses, and then adds – 'Simulated'. He quickly proves incapable of responding to situations that do not follow his simulation training.

But in the slightly less scientised and fictionalised present the proliferation of war simulations has engendered some immediate policy concerns. Simulations have given rise to important intertexts of strategic power and popular culture. Take Tom Clancy and his intertextual relationship to war games. The best non-fictional book on the subject, *War Games: The Secret World of the Creators, Players, and Policy-makers Rehearsing World War III Today* written by Thomas Allen (1987), sports a cover blurb by Tom Clancy who writes that it 'will be the standard work on the subject for the next ten years'. Clancy's first bestseller, *Red October*, has a hyperbolic blurb from former President Reagan. His second novel, *Red Storm Rising*, a thinly fictionalised mosaic of NATO war games, was authoritatively cited by Vice-President Quayle in a foreign policy speech to prove that the USA needs an anti-satellite capability. His third novel, *The Cardinal of the Kremlin*, in which Clancy plots the plight of a mole in the Kremlin, affirms the need to reconstruct the impermeable borders of the sovereign state with Star Wars. And in his fourth, *Patriot Games*, Clancy magnifies the threat of terrorism to prove that state counter-terrorism works, a view endorsed by Secretary of Defense Weinberger in a laudatory review of the book for the *Wall Street Journal* – which was then reprinted in the Pentagon's *Current News* for the edification of the 7,000-odd Defense and State Department officials who make up its readership. Taken together, Clancy's novels stand out as strategic simulations. Jammed with technical detail and seductive ordnance, devoid of recognisably human characters, and obliquely linked to historical events, they have become the perfect free-floating intertext for saving the reality principle of the national security state: namely, that the sovereign state's boundaries, like those between fiction and fact, simulation and reality, can once again be made impermeable to the Soviet threat, the terrorist attack and even the launch of ICBMs.

At a more mundane level, simulations have acquired a very important budgetary function. After interviews with fast-track colonels from the various war colleges and with modellers from the RAND Corporation, I discovered that there is a very high demand for the best modellers, not just, as one would expect, to provide the best possible preparation for battle, but to convince the essential sub-committees of the Congress where funds should best be allocated. The different services compete to present the most detailed and technically ornate simulation – down to the number of roles of computer paper needed in the unlikely event of a Soviet invasion of Europe – to get a heftier chunk of the budgetary pie. As the arms race shows signs of winding down, the simulation race is speeding up. It would seem that war gaming has been joined, if not supplanted, by gaming wars.

There is of course a fundamental and ultimate difference between warring and gaming: people die in wars. This fact must temper any neo-Luddite rant against the computer simulation of war. Surely a properly executed simulation can play an important edifying role in alerting us to the horrors of war. It has been said that Ronald Reagan's participation in a DEFCON alert simulation, which included an evacuation from Washington, DC, noticeably altered his attitude toward strategic issues and arms control. And as many players of war games would be quick to claim, by preparing nation-states for future wars, they might help to keep the peace: *qui desiderat pacem, praeparet bellum*.

Perhaps the best hope to be derived from the pervasive simulation of war is that we might prolong the preparation and postpone the execution of war indefinitely. Perhaps NATO and Warsaw Pact talks on 'open battlefields' will soon follow the current ones on 'open skies', resulting in not only permission to watch but to participate in each other's war games. Perhaps Fort Irwin's fictitious 197th Krasnovian Motorized Rifle Regiment will finally meet its fictitious match, the Soviet brigade pretending to be American at their own National Training Center in the Carpathian Mountains.

Of course, this is to minimise grossly the possibility of nuclear and conventional accidents, nationalist conflicts and proxy wars. But can we imagine a hundred years from now, when the time for a bicentenary celebration approaches, that strategists will be so far *inside* the simulation of war that they will neither feel a nostalgia for 'real' war nor be able to distinguish it from some 'original' model? Should we be horrified by the thought? Or just game on?

Bibliography

Abbot, H. Porter (1988) 'Autobiography, Autography, Fiction: Groundwork for a Taxonomy of Textual Categories', *New Literary History* 19: 597–615.

Allardt, Erik (1956) 'Social struktur och politisk aktivitet. En studie av väljaraktiviteten vid riksdagsvalen i Finland 1945–54', *Skrifter utgivna av Nyliberala Studentförbundet* no. 15, Helsingfors: Söderströms.

Allardt, Erik and Kettil Bruun (1956) 'Characteristics of the Finnish Non-Voter', *Transactions of the Westermarck Society* 3: 55–76.

Allardt, Erik and Pertti Pesonen (1960) *Citizen Participation in Political Life in Finland*. Publication no. 7 of the Institute of Sociology, University of Helsinki.

Allen, Thomas (1987) *War Games: The Secret World of the Creators, Players, and Policy-makers Rehearsing World War III Today*, New York: McGraw-Hill.

Almond, G.A. and S. Verba (1965) *The Civic Culture*, Boston MA and Toronto: Little, Brown.

Anderson, Benedict (1988) *Die Erfindung der Nation* (*Imagined Communities: Reflections on the Origin and Spread of Nationalism*), trans. B. Burkhard, Frankfurt am Main: Campus Verlag.

——(1991) *Imagined Communities*, rev. edn, London: Verso.

Aquinas, T. (1922) *Summa Theologica*, trans. Fathers of the English Dominican Province, London: Burns, Oates & Washbourne.

Arendt, Hannah (1958) *The Human Condition*, Chicago and London: University of Chicago Press.

——(1958) *Vita Activa*, German translation 1981, Munich: Piper.

Aristoteles (1980) *Rhetorik*, trans. Franz G. Sieveke, Munich: Wilhelm Fink Verlag.

Aristotle (1992) *The Politics*, trans. T.J. Saunders, Harmondsworth: Penguin.

Augustine, St (1961) *Confessions*, trans. R.S. Pine-Coffin, Harmondsworth: Penguin.

Austin, J.L. (1990) *How To Do Things With Words*, ed. J.O. Urmson and Marina Sbisa, Oxford: Oxford University Press.

Azaryahu, Maoz (1990) 'Renaming the Past: Changes in "City Text" in Germany and Austria, 1945–1947', *History and Memory* 2: 32–53.

Ball, Terence (1987) *Idioms of Inquiry: Critique and Renewal in Political Science*, Albany: State University of New York Press.

Banfield, E.C. (1958) *The Moral Basis of a Backward Society*, New York: Free Press.

Baudrillard, Jean (1988) *Selected Writings*, ed. Mark Poster, Cambridge: Polity.

Bauman, Zygmunt (1987) *Legislators and Interpreters*, Cambridge: Polity.

Benjamin, Walter (1969) *Illuminationen*, Frankfurth am Main: Suhrkamp.

——(1980) *Über den Begriff der Geschichte*, in *Illuminationen*, pp. 251–61, first published 1940, Frankfurt am Main: Suhrkamp.

——(1983) *Das Passagen-Werk*, ed. Rolf Tiedemann, Frankfurt am Main: Suhrkamp.

Bernstein, R.J. (1976) *The Restructuring of Social and Political Theory*, Oxford: Basil Blackwell.

Bleicher, Josef (1980) *Contemporary Hermeneutics*, London: Routledge.

Bloch, Ernst (1985) *Erbschaft dieser Zeit*, first published 1935, Frankfurt am Main: Suhrkamp.

Boyne, Roy and Ali Rattansi (1990) *Postmodernism and Society*, Basingstoke: Macmillan Education.

Brandt, Willy (1983) 'Ich bin besorgt', *Die Zeit* 16 December 1983.

Brownmiller, Susan (1975) *Against our Will: Men, Women and Rape*, London: Secker & Warburg.

Bruner, Jerome (1990) *Acts of Meaning*, Cambridge MA: Harvard University Press.

Bruss, Elisabeth (1976) *Autobiographical Acts: The Changing Situation of a Literary Genre*, Baltimore and London: The Johns Hopkins University Press.

Bryson, V. (1994) *Feminist Political Theory*, London: Macmillan.

Burke, Kenneth (1945) *A Grammar of Motives*, New York: Prentice Hall.

——(1984) *Attitudes toward History*, 3rd edn, Berkeley CA: University of California Press.

Burman, Pauli (1957) 'Helsinki poliittisena käyttäytymisalueena', unpublished Master's thesis, University of Helsinki.

Carrithers, Michael, Steven Collins and Steven Lukes (1985) *The Category of the Person: Anthropology, Philosophy, History*, Cambridge: Cambridge University Press.

Chatman, S. (1978) *Story and Discourse*, Ithaca NY: Cornell University Press.

Cohen, A.P. (1985) *The Symbolic Reconstruction of Community*, London: Ellis Horwood.

Connolly, William E. (1991) *Identity/Difference: Democratic Negotiations of Political Paradox*, Ithaca NY: Cornell University Press.

Cox, James M. (1989) *Recovering Literature's Lost Ground: Essays in American Autobiography*, Baton Rouge LA: Louisiana State University Press.

Culler, J. (1975) *Structuralist Poetics*, London: Routledge & Kegan Paul.

Dahrendorf, Ralph (1990) *Reflections on the Revolution in Europe*, London: Chatto.

Daly, Mary (1984) *Pure Lust: Elemental Feminist Philosophy*, London: The Women's Press.

Davidson, Arnold I. (1986) 'Archaeology, Genealogy, Ethics', in David Couzens Hoy (ed.), *Foucault: A Critical Reader*, pp. 221–34, Oxford: Basil Blackwell.

De Lauretis, Teresa (1987) *Technologies of Gender: Essays on Theory, Film and Fiction*, London: Macmillan.

Deleuze, Gilles (1986) *Foucault*, Paris: Editions de Minuit.

Denzin, Norman K. (1989) *Interpretive Interactionism*, London: Sage.

Dreyfus, Hubert L. and Paul Rabinow (1982) *Michel Foucault: Beyond Structuralism and Hermeneutics*, Chicago: University of Chicago Press.

Drury, Allen (1959) *Advise and Consent*, Garden City: Doubleday.

Dryzek, J.S. and J. Berejikian (1993) 'Reconstructive Democratic Theory', *American Political Science Review* 87: 48–59.

Dworkin, Andrea (1981) *Pornography: Men Possessing Women*, London: The Women's Press.

——(1988) *Letters from a War Zone*, Harmondsworth: Penguin.

Dworkin, Ronald (1991) 'Justice for Clarence Thomas', *New York Review of Books* 38 (7 November).

Edelman, M. (1971) *Politics as Symbolic Action*, Chicago: Markan.

Edmondson, Ricca (1984) *Rhetoric in Sociology*, London: Macmillan.

Elias, Norbert (1989) *Studien über die Deutschen*, Frankfurt am Main: Suhrkamp.

Elster, Jon (1986) *The Multiple Self*, Cambridge: Cambridge University Press.

Enzensberger, Hans Magnus (1973) 'Revolutionstourismus', in *Palaver: Politische Überlegungen*, pp. 130–68, Frankfurt am Main: Suhrkamp.

——(1982) 'Resozismus: Der höchste Studium der Unterentwicklung', in *Politische Brosamen*, pp. 53–74, Frankfurt am Main: Suhrkamp.

——(1987) *Ach Europa!*, Frankfurt am Main: Suhrkamp.

——(1988) *Mittelmaß und Wahn*, Frankfurt am Main: Suhrkamp.

——(1989a) *Europe, Europe*, London: Nicholson.

——(1989b) 'Europa und Brüssel', in *Der fliegende Robert*, pp. 117–25, Frankfurt am Main: Suhrkamp.

Eribon, Didier (1994) *Michel Foucault et ses contemporains*, Paris: Fayard.

Felski, Rita (1989) 'Feminist Theory and Social Change', *Theory, Culture and Society* 6: 219–40.

Ferguson, Priscilla Parkhurst (1988) 'Reading City Streets', *The French Review* 61: 386–97.

Firestone, Shulamith (1972) *The Dialectic of Sex*, New York: Bantam.

Foucault, M. (1972a) *The Archaeology of Knowledge*, first published 1969, New York: Pantheon.

——(1972b) 'The Discourse on Language', in *The Archaeology of Knowledge*, first published 1971, New York: Pantheon.

——(1972c) *The Archaeology of Knowledge*, London: Tavistock.

——(1978) *The History of Sexuality*, vol. 1: *An Introduction*, first published 1976, New York: Pantheon.

——(1985) *The History of Sexuality*, vol. 2: *The Use of Pleasure*, first published 1984, New York: Pantheon.

——(1986a) 'Nietzsche, Genealogy, History', in Paul Rabinow (ed.), *The Foucault Reader*, pp. 76–100, first published 1971, New York: Pantheon.

——(1986b) 'On the Genealogy of Ethics: An Overview of Work in

Progress', in Paul Rabinow (ed.), *The Foucault Reader*, pp. 340–72, New York: Pantheon.

——(1986c) 'Nietzsche, Freud, Marx', *Critical Text* 3: 1–5.

——(1988) *The History of Sexuality*, vol. 3: *Care of the Self*, first published 1984, London: Allen Lane.

——(1994a) 'Nietzsche, Freud, Marx', in *Dits et écrits 1954–1988 par Michel Foucault*, vol. 1, pp. 564–79, first published 1967, Paris: Gallimard.

——(1994b) 'Non au sexe roi', in *Dits et écrits 1954–1988 par Michel Foucault*, vol. 3, pp. 256–71, first published 1977, Paris: Gallimard.

——(1994c) 'Sexualité et politique', in *Dits et écrits 1954–1988 par Michel Foucault*, vol. 4, pp. 522–31, first published 1978, Paris: Gallimard.

Fraser, Ronald (ed.) (1988) *1968: A Student Generation in Revolt*, New York: Pantheon.

Friday, Nancy (1973) *My Secret Garden: Women's Sexual Fantasies*, New York: Pocket Books.

——(1975) *Forbidden Flowers: More Women's Sexual Fantasies*, New York: Pocket Books.

——(1980) *Men in Love: Men's Sexual Fantasies – The Triumph of Love over Rage*, New York: Dell.

Friedman, Susan Stanford (1988) 'Women's Autobiographical Selves: Theory and Practice', in Shari Benstock (ed.), *The Private Self: Theory and Practice of Women's Autobiographical Writings*, pp. 34–62, London: Routledge.

Gadamer, Hans-Georg (1975) *Wahrheit und Methode*, Tübingen: Mohr.

Galtung, J. (1973) *The European Community: A Superpower in the Making*, Oslo: Universitetsverlaget.

Garton Ash, Timothy (1989) *The Uses of Adversity*, Harmondsworth: Penguin.

——(1990) *We The People*, Harmondsworth: Penguin.

Garvin, T. (1988) 'The Politics of Denial and Cultural Defense: The Referenda of 1983 and 1986 in Context', *Irish Review* 3: 1–7.

Gates, Henry Lewis (1988) 'James Gronniosaw and the Trope of the Talking Book', in James Olney (ed.), *Studies in Autobiography*, pp. 51–72, New York: Oxford University Press.

Geertz, Clifford (1973) *The Interpretation of Cultures: Selected Essays*, New York: Basic Books.

——(1975) *The Interpretation of Cultures*, London: Hutchinson.

Gellner, Ernest (1964) *Thought and Change*, London: Weidenfeld & Nicolson.

Giddens, Anthony (1982) *Profiles and Critiques in Social Theory*, London: Macmillan.

——(1987) *Social Theory Today*, Cambridge: Polity.

——(1992) *The Transformation of Intimacy: Sexuality, Love and Eroticism in Modern Societies*, Cambridge: Polity.

Gordon, Colin (ed.) (1980) *Power/Knowledge: Selected Interviews and Other Writings by Michel Foucault 1972–1977*, Brighton: Harvester.

Griffin, Charles J.G. (1990) 'The Rhetoric of Forms in Conversion Narratives', *Quarterly Journal of Speech* 76: 152–63.

Griffin, Susan (1981) *Pornography and Silence: Culture's Revenge Against Women*, London: The Women's Press.

Gusdorf, Georges (1980) 'Condition and Limits of Autobiography', in James Olney (ed.), *Autobiography: Essays Theoretical and Critical*, pp. 28–48, first published 1956, Princeton NJ: Princeton University Press.

Gusfield, Joseph (1976) 'The Literary Rhetoric of Science: Comedy and Pathos in Drinking Driver Research', *American Sociological Review* 41: 16–34.

Habermas, J. (1979) *Communication and the Evolution of Society*, London: Heinemann.

——(1990) *Die nachholende Revolution*, Frankfurt am Main: Suhrkamp.

Hacking, Ian (1991) 'How Should We Do The History of Statistics?', in Graham Burchell, Colin Gordon and Peter Miller (eds), *The Foucault Effect: Studies in Governmentality*, pp. 181–96, London: Harvester Wheatsheaf.

Hall, Stuart (1989) *Ausgewählte Schriften: Ideologie, Kultur, Medien, Neue Rechte, Rassismus*, ed. Nora Rätzel, Hamburg: Argument Verlag.

Hamm, Bernd (1992) 'Europe – A Challenge to the Social Sciences', *International Social Science Journal* 131: 3–22.

Haraway, Donna J. (1991) *Simians, Cyborgs, and Women: The Reinvention of Nature*, London: Free Association Books.

Hiller, Kurt (1973) 'Literaturpolitik', in *Die Weisheit der Langeweile*, pp. 90–4, first published 1911, Nendeln: Kraus.

Hite, Shere (1976) *The Hite Report on Female Sexuality*, New York: Dell.

——(1981) *The Hite Report on Male Sexuality*, New York: Ballantine.

——(1987) *Women and Love: The Hite Report on Love, Passion and Emotional Violence*, New York: St Martin's Press.

——(1994) *The Hite Report on the Family: Growing Up Under Patriarchy*, London: Bloomsbury.

Hitler, Adolf (1933) *Mein Kampf*, Munich: Franz Feher.

Hobbes, T. (1968) *Leviathan*, ed. C.B. McPherson, Harmondsworth: Penguin.

Hobsbawm, Eric and Terence Ranger (eds) (1983) *The Invention of Tradition*, Cambridge: Cambridge University Press.

Hyvärinen, Matti (1992) 'Narrative Analysis and Political Autobiography', *Journal of Political Science* 20: 51–70.

——(1994) *Viimeiset taistot* (*The Last Fights*), Tampere: Vastapaino.

Jackson, Margaret (1994) *The Real Facts of Life: Feminism and the Politics of Sexuality*, London: Taylor & Francis.

Jansson, Jan-Magnus (1966) 'Defining Political Science: Some Basic Reflections', *Scandinavian Political Studies* 1: 13–24.

Kinsey, Alfred C., Wordell B. Pomeroy and Clyde B. Martin (1949) *Sexual Behaviour in the Human Male*, Philadelphia PA: Saunders.

Kinsey, Alfred C. and Staff of the Institute for Sex Research, Indiana University (1953) *Sexual Behaviour in the Human Female*, Philadelphia PA: Saunders.

Koedt, Anne (1973) 'The Myth of the Vaginal Orgasm', in Anne Koedt, Ellen Levine and Anita Rapone (eds), *Radical Feminism*, pp. 28–53, New York: New York Times Books.

Koselleck, Reinhart (1979) *Vergangene Zukunft*, Frankfurt am Main: Suhrkamp.

Kraus, Karl (1989) *Dritte Walpurgisnacht*, first published 1933, Frankfurt am Main: Suhrkamp.

Kritzman, Lawrence D. (ed.) (1988) *Michel Foucault: Politics, Philosophy, Culture – Interviews and Other Writings*, London: Routledge.

Labov, William (1972) *Language in the Inner City: Studies in the Black English Vernacular*, Philadelphia PA: University of Pennsylvania Press.

Laqueur, Thomas W. (1989) 'Amor Veneris, vel Dulcedo Appeletur', in Michel Feher, Ramona Naddaff and Nadia Tazi (eds), *Fragments for a History of the Human Body*, Part Three, pp. 90–131, New York: Zone.

Lavoie, Don (1990) *Economics and Hermeneutics*, London: Routledge.

Lehto, O. (1959) 'Oulun kaupunki poliittisena käyttäytymisalueena', unpublished Master's thesis, University of Helsinki.

Lévi-Strauss, C. (1963) *Structural Anthropology*, New York: Basic Books.

Lewis, Bernard (1975) *History Remembered, Recovered, Invented*, Princeton NJ: Princeton University Press.

Linde, Charlotte (1993) *Life Stories: The Creation of Coherence*, New York: Oxford University Press.

Lipgens, Walter (ed.) (1985) *Documents on the History of European Integration*, vol. 1: *Continental Plans for European Union 1939–45*, vol. 2: *Plans for European Union in Great Britain and in Exile*, Berlin: de Gruyter.

Lloyd, G. (1993) *The Man of Reason*, London: Routledge.

Locke, J. (1947) *Two Treatises of Civil Government*, ed. T.L. Hafner, New York: Cook Press.

Lowenthal, David (1985) *The Past is a Foreign Country*, Cambridge: Cambridge University Press.

Luhmann, Niklas (1990) *Political Theory in the Welfare State*, trans. John Bednarz Jr., Berlin: de Gruyter.

Luostarinen, Heikki and Esa Väliverronen (1991) *Tekstinsyöjät: Yhteiskuntatieteellisen tutkimuksen lukutaidosta*, Tampere: Vastapaino.

Lüsenbrink, Hans-Jürgen and Rolf Reichardt (1990) *Die 'Bastille': Zur Symbolgeschichte von Herrschaft und Freiheit*, Frankfurt am Main: Fischer Verlag.

Machiavelli, N. (1970a) *The History of Florence and Other Selections*, trans. and ed. M.P. Gilmore, New York: Washington Square Press.

——(1970b) *The Discourses*, ed. Bernard Crick, Harmondsworth: Penguin.

Maier, Charles S. (1987) 'The Politics of Time: Changing Paradigms of Collective Time and Private Time in the Modern Era', in Charles S. Maier (ed.), *Changing Boundaries of the Political*, pp. 157–75, Cambridge: Cambridge University Press.

Marx, Karl (1978) *The Eighteenth Brumaire of Louis Bonaparte*, in Robert C. Tucker (ed.), *The Marx–Engels Reader*, New York: W.W. Norton.

Mason, Mary G. (1980) 'The Other Voice: Autobiographies of Women Writers', in James Olney (ed.), *Autobiography: Essays Theoretical and Critical*, pp. 207–35, Princeton NJ: Princeton University Press.

Masters, William and Virginia Johnson (1970) *Human Sexual Inadequacy*, Boston MA: Little, Brown.

Meana, Ripa di (1987) 'Foreword', in European Commission, *A Fresh Boost for Culture in the Community: Supplement*, April 1987.

Melone, Albert *et al.* (1992) 'Too Little Advice, Senatorial Responsibility, and Confirmation Politics', *Judicature* 75: 187–92.

Mill, J.S. (1980) *On Liberty and Other Essays*, ed. J. Gray, Oxford: Oxford University Press.

Miller, Nancy K. (1994) 'Representing Others: Gender and the Subjects of Autobiography', *Differences: A Journal of Feminist Cultural Studies* 6: 1–27.

Miller, S. (1988) *Verschlossene Gesellschaft*, Hamburg: Rowohlt. English trans. *Painted in Blood: Understanding the European Mind*, New York: Atheneum.

Millet, Kate (1970) *Sexual Politics*, London: Virago.

Mishler, Elliot G. (1986) *Research Interviewing: Context and Narrative*, Cambridge MA: Harvard University Press.

Monnet, Jean (1978) *Memoirs*, New York: Doubleday.

Morin, Edgar (1987) *Penser l'Europe*, Paris: Gallimard.

Mottier, Véronique (1994) 'La mise en discours de la sexualité: le féminisme à la recherche de stratégies', *Swiss Yearbook of Political Science* 34: 79–98.

Murphy, John W. (1989) *Postmodern Social Analysis and Criticism*, New York: Greenwood.

Murray, Kevin (1989) 'The Construction of Identity in the Narratives of Romance and Comedy', in John Shotter and Kenneth J. Gergen (eds), *Texts of Identity*, pp. 176–205, London: Sage.

Nousiainen, Jaakko (1956) *Kommunismi Kuopion läänissä. Ekologinen tutkimus kommunismin joukkokannatukseen vaikuttavista tekijöistä Pohjois-Savossa ja Pohjois-Karjalassa*, Joensuu: Pohjois-Karjalan Kirjapaino Oy.

——(1958) 'Pohjois-Karjala poliittisena käyttäytymisalueena', *Puukello* no. 2.

——(1960) 'Poliittisen ekologian periaatteita ja menetelmiä', *Politiikka* 3: 123–38.

O'Leary, C. and T. Heskith (1988) 'The Irish Abortion and Divorce Referendum Campaigns', *Irish Political Studies* 3: 43–62.

Palonen, Kari (1989) 'Korrekturen zur Geschichte von "Politisierung"', *Archiv für Begriffsgeschichte* 30: 224–34.

——(1993a) 'Introduction: From Policy and Polity to Politicking and Politicization', in Kari Palonen and Tuija Parvikko (eds), *Reading the Political*, pp. 6–16, Helsinki: FPSA.

——(1993b) 'Reading Street Names Politically', in Kari Palonen and Tuija Parvikko (eds), *Reading the Political*, pp. 103–21, Helsinki: FPSA.

Perelman, C. and L. Olbrechts-Tyteca (1971) *The New Rhetoric: A Treatise on Argumentation*, Notre Dame IN: University of Notre Dame Press.

Pesonen, Pertti (1958a) *Valitsijamiesvaalien ylioppilasäänestäjät*, Helsinki: Vammalan Kirjapaino.

——(1958b) 'Vaalidemokratia ja tutkimus', *Suomalainen Suomi* 26: 369–71.

——(1960a) 'The Voting Behaviour of Finnish Students', in *Democracy in Finland 1960*, pp. 93–104, Helsinki: Finnish Political Science Association.

——(1960b) 'Yksilö poliittisessa järjestelmässä', *Suomalainen Suomi* 28: 536–40.
——(1961) 'Valtiotieteilijäin viides maailmankongressi', *Turun yliopiston valtio-opin laitos, eripainossarja*, A, no. 4.
——(1962) *Studies on Finnish Political Behaviour*, in Austin Ranney (ed.), *Essays on the Behavioral Study of Politics*, pp. 217–34, Urbana IL: University of Illinois Press.
——(1964) 'Puoluekannan omaksuminen', *Aamulehti* 1. ja 7. toukok., Tampere: Tampereen Kirjapaino Oy.
——(1965) *Valtuutus kansalta, Tutkimus Tampereen vaalioikeutetuista, vaalikampanjasta ja äänestyskäyttäytymisestä*, Porvoo: WSOY.
——(ed.) (1972) *Protestivaalit, nuorisovaalit; Tutkielmia kansanedustajien vaaleista 1966, 1970 ja 1972*, Helsinki: Ylioppilastuki.
Pesonen, Pertti and Rantala Onni (1967) 'Current Election Studies in Finland', *Tampereen yliopisto, Politiikan tutkimuksen laitos, tutkielmia*, no. 5.
Pietilä, Kauko and Klaus Sondermann (1994) *Sanomalehden yhteiskunta*, Tampere: Vastapaino.
Pitkin, H.F. (1987) *Fortune is a Woman*, Berkeley CA: University of California Press.
Poster, Mark (1986) 'Foucault and the Tyranny of Greece', in David Couzens Hoy (ed.), *Foucault: A Critical Reader*, pp. 205–20, Oxford: Basil Blackwell.
Potter, J. and M. Wetherell (1987) *Discourse and Social Psychology: Beyond Attitudes and Behaviour*, London: Sage.
Procter, David (1991) *Enacting Political Culture: Rhetorical Transformations of Liberty Weekend 1986*, New York: Praeger.
Pusch, Luise F. (1990) 'Lila Lotta Lesbeton', in *Alle Menschen werden Schwestern*, pp. 61–79, Frankfurt am Main: Suhrkamp.
Rahkonen, Jaakko (1961) 'Huomioita Turun kaupungin sanomalehtilukusalien käytöstä', *Turun yliopiston valtio-opin laitos, eripainossarja* A, no. 2.
Rantala, Onni (1956) *Konservatiivinen puolueyhteisö. Tutkimus Satakunnan kansallisliiton jäsenistön yhteiskunnallisen rakenteen vaikutuksesta jäsenyhteisöön ja sen toimintaan*, Vammala: Vammalan Kirjapaino.
——(1962) 'Poliittisen regionalismin syntyselityksiä', *Politiikka* 4: 158–65.
Rich, Adrienne (1983) 'Compulsory Heterosexuality and Lesbian Existence', in Elizabeth Abel and Emily K. Abel (eds), *The Signs Reader: Women, Gender and Scholarship*, Chicago: University of Chicago Press.
Ricoeur, P. (1974) *The Conflict of Interpretations*, ed. D. Ihde, Evanston IL: Northwestern University Press.
——(1989) *Hermeneutics and the Human Sciences*, ed. J.B. Thompson, Cambridge: Cambridge University Press.
Rorty, Richard (1989) *Contingency, Irony, and Solidarity*, Cambridge: Cambridge University Press.
Rose, N. (1990) *Governing the Soul: The Shaping of the Private Self*, London: Routledge.
Rousseau, Jean-Jacques (1979) *Reveries of the Solitary Walker*, trans. Peter France, Harmondsworth: Penguin.

Ryan, Michael (1988) 'Postmodern Politics', *Theory, Culture and Society* 5: 559–76.
Saxonhouse, A.W. (1985) *Women in the History of Political Thought*, New York: Praeger.
Schmidt, Helmut (1991) *Die Zeit*, 230: 17.
Schmitt, Carl (1933) *Der Begriff des Politischen*, Berlin: Duncker.
Schulte, Hagen (1990) *Die Wiederkehr Europas*, Berlin: Siedler Verlag.
Schwengel, Hermann (1989) 'European Way of Life', in *Jahrbuch für Europäische Kulturpolitik, Kulturpolitische Gesellschaft*, pp. 15–37, Köln: Volksblatt Verlag.
Shanks, Michael and Christopher Tilly (1987) *Social Theory and Archaeology*, Cambridge: Polity.
Shapiro, Michael (1986) 'Metaphor in the Philosophy of the Social Sciences', *Cultural Critique* 2: 191–214.
Sheehan, J. (1985) 'The Problem of the Nation in German History', in *Die Rolle der Nation in der Deutschen Geschichte und Gegenwart*, ed. O. Büsch and J. Sheehan, pp. 3–20, Berlin: Colloquium Verlag.
Sherfey, Mary (1972) *The Nature and Evolution of Female Sexuality*, New York: Random House.
Siltanen, Janet and Michelle Stanworth (1984) *Women and the Public Sphere: A Critique of Sociology and Politics*, London: Hutchinson.
Simmel, Georg (1987) *Das individuelle Gesetz: Philosophische Exkurse*, ed. M. Landmann, Frankfurt am Main: Suhrkamp.
Slater, P.E. (1968) *The Glory of Hera*, Boston MA: Beacon Press.
Sondermann, Klaus (1992) *Die Nation als Trivialität und als Subjekt*, in *Die Wanderratten: Randbemerkungen zur Migration*, Jyväskylä University Library.
Spinelli, A. (1966) *The Eurocrats: Conflict and Crisis in the European Community*, Baltimore MD: Johns Hopkins University Press.
Stölting, Erhard (1988) 'Die Wiedervereinigung als Droge', in *Vom der Gnade der geschenkten Nation*, pp. 200–16, ed. Hajo Funke, Nördlingen: Wagner.
Summa, Hilkka (1990) 'Retoriikka hallinnon ja politiikan käytännöissä ja tutkimuksessa', mimeo.
Tannen, Deborah (1979) 'What's in a Frame?', in Roy O. Freedle (ed.), *New Directions in Discourse Processing*, pp. 137–81, Norwood NJ: Ablex.
Teljo, Jussi (1950) 'Valtio-opin tehtävät ja menetelmät', *Suomalainen Suomi* 18: 14–18.
Thiele, Leslie Paul (1990) 'The Agony of Politics: The Nietzschean Roots of Foucault's Thought', *American Political Science Review* 84: 907–25.
Thompson, J.B. (1990) *Ideology and Modern Culture*, Cambridge: Polity.
Touraine, Alain (1981) *The Voice and the Eye*, Cambridge: Cambridge University Press.
Tully, James (1988) *Meaning and Context: Quentin Skinner and His Critics*, Cambridge: Polity.
Visker, Rudi (1990) *Genealogie als kritiek: Michel Foucault en de menswetenschappen*, Den Haag: Boom.
Voigt, Klaus (1988) *Friedenssicherung und europäische Einigung: Ideen des deutschen Exils 1939–1945*, Frankfurt am Main: Fischer Verlag.

Weber, Max (1980) 'Die Stadt', in *Wirtschaft und Gesellschaft*, pp. 727–814, first published 1921, Tübingen: Mohr.
——(1994) 'Politik als Beruf', in *Max-Weber-Studienausgabe*, vol. I/17, pp. 35–80, first published 1919, Tübingen: Mohr.
Weeks, Jeffrey (1989) *Sex, Politics and Society: The Regulation of Sexuality since 1800*, New York: Longman.
Wohlrab-Sahr, Monika (1992) 'Conversion Processes: Paradigm Shifts and the Reconstruction of Biography', unpublished paper, XIII World Congress of Sociology, 18–23 July 1994, Bielefeld, Germany.
Woolgar, Steve (ed.) (1988) *Knowledge and Reflexivity: New Frontiers in the Sociology of Knowledge*, London: Sage.

Index